Aviation Communication and Flight Radio *for Helicopter Pilots*

About this Publication

Document Name:

Aviation Communication and Flight Radio

Series:

For Helicopter Pilots

Edition:

First published 2011, Ninth Edition, January 2022

Principal Author:

Mike Becker, ATPL(H), FIR, FER, Diploma (Training and Assessment)

Editor:

Bev Austen, BTech(CompSt), MEd(DTL)

Copyright

Copyright © 2022 Becker Helicopter Services Pty Ltd

Photos and Illustrations

The majority of photos and illustrations in this document have been sourced from Becker Helicopter Services Pty Ltd. The remainder is taken from the internet from various sources; Every effort has been made to ensure images with Creative Commons Licences have been used and appropriate attribution provided.

Disclaimer

Nothing in this text supersedes any operational documents issued by any civil aviation authority or regulatory body, aircraft, engine, and avionics manufacturers, or the operators of aircraft throughout the world. No responsibility is taken for the interpretation and application of the information contained in this document. Managing the safety of the aircraft is the sole responsibility of the pilot-in-command.

Every possible effort has been made to establish the accuracy of the information contained in this book, however, the author, Becker Helicopter Services Pty Ltd, accept no responsibility for errors or omissions.

The Publisher and the Author make no representations or warranties for the accuracy or completeness of the contents of this work and specifically disclaim all warranties, including without limitation warranties of fitness for a particular purpose. No warranty may be created or extended by sales or promotional materials. The advice and strategies contained herein may not be suitable for every situation. This work is sold with the understanding that the author is not engaged in rendering legal, accounting, or other professional services. If professional assistance is required, the services of a competent professional person should be sought. Neither the Publisher nor the Author shall be liable for damages arising therefrom.

The fact that an organisation or website is referred to in this work as a citation and/or a potential source of further information does not mean that the author or the Publisher endorses the information the organisation or website may provide or recommendations it may make. Further, readers should be aware that internet websites listed in this work may have changed or disappeared between when this work was written and when it is read.

Contents

About this Publication 1
Contents 2
About this Book 7
About the Author 8

Introduction to Flight Radio 9
    Factors that help you communicate 9
    Face to-face vs radio communication 10
    Elements of An Effective Radio Call 11
    What is radio? 12
        History 12
        Components 12
    Components of a Radio 13

Flight Radio Operator Rules 16
    ICAO English levels 16
        Level 6: Expert 16
        Level 5: Extended 17
        Level 4: Operational 17
        Level 3: Pre-Operational 18
        Level 2: Elementary 18
        Level 1: Pre-Elementary 18
    Flight Radio Operator Rules in Australia 19
    Training Course 20
        Assessment 20
        Competency scale 20
        Applicability 20
        Requirements 20
        Rating scale 21
            Level 6 - Expert 21
            Level 5 – Extended 21
            Level 4 – Operational 22

Standard Words and Phrases 23
    Phonetic Alphabet 24
    Numbers 25
    Measurements 26
        Vertical Measurements (Height) 26
        Horizontal Measurements (Visibility - Distance) 26
        Horizontal Measurements (Distances) 26
        Speed 27
        Headings and Direction 27
    Time in Aviation 28
        Local Time 28
        Daylight Saving Time 28
        Local Time in the USA 28
        Local Time in Australia 29
        Transmitting Time 30
    Standard Words and Phrases 31
    Abbreviations, Acronym, and Mnemonics 33

   Abbreviations (Abb)..33
    Method of Abbreviation..33
    City Names and Airport Codes 34
  Acronyms 34
  Mnemonics 35
  Combinations 36
 Callsigns and Identifiers 37
  Aircraft Registration Callsigns 37
  Vehicle Callsigns 38
  Runways and Taxiways 38
 Standard shorthand 39

Understanding Airspace 40

 Australian Flight Information Region 40
 Australian Communication Centres 41
 Classes of Airspace 42
 Military Airspace 43
 Air Defence Identification Zone (ADIZ) 44
 Prohibited, Restricted and Danger (PRD) Areas..45
  Restricted Areas 45
  Danger 47
 Difference between CTA and CTR 48
  Control Area (CTA) 48
  Control Zones (CTR) 48
 Implied Clearance...49
 Radar at Airports 51
  Radar environment...51
  Non-Radar Environment 52

Maps and Charts..53

 Common abbreviations used on the maps...53
 Understanding the Map Markings 54
 Review of the Sunshine Coast VTC 57
 Review of the Brisbane VNC 58

Radio Procedures Overview...59

 Types of Radio Calls 59
 Procedure...59
 Pronunciation and Voice Control 60
 Initiating a Call..60
 Responding to a Call 61
 Established Communication...61
 Corrections...61
 Clearances and Readbacks 62

Who to call...63

 Recorded messages 63
  Automatic Terminal Information Service (ATIS)..64
  Aerodrome Weather Information: AWIS or AWIB 65
  Automatic Enroute Information Service (AERIS) 66
 Airways Clearance Delivery (ACD) 66
 Surface Movement Control (Ground) - SMC (Ground) 67
 Tower Controller 67

- Departures and Approach 68
- Flight Information Area (FIA) 70
- Flight Information Service (FIS) 70
- Unicom 71
- Outside controlled airspace (OCTA) 71
- Non-towered aerodromes 71
  - Certified aerodrome 72
  - Un-certified aerodrome 72
  - Registered aerodrome 72
- Standard CTAF procedures 73
- Tower Operating Hours 74
- Summary of Who to Call 74

When to call 75
- ATIS 75
- Airways Clearance Delivery (ACD) 75
- SMC (Surface Movement Control) referred to as Ground (GND) 75
- Tower (TWR) 75
- Departures and Approach 75
- Flight Information Area (FIA) 76
- Unicom 76
- Non-towered aerodrome 76

How to call 77
- Techniques when making a call 77
  - Speak Slowly 77
  - Articulate your words 77
  - Volume 77
  - Speak into the microphone 77
  - Listen 77
- Broadcasts 78
- Report 78
- Calls 78
- What to say 79
- Readback 82
- Over Transmissions 82
- Clipped Transmissions 83
- Establish Comms 83
- Courtesy Calls 84

Readability scale 86
- Readability scale format: single- or double-digit 86
  - Using the single-digit method 86
  - Using the double-digit method: 86
- When to use the readability scale 87

When the Radio Fails 88
- Troubleshooting Radio Failure 88
- Radio Failure Procedures 89
- Radio Failure Inside Controlled Airspace 90
- Radio Failure Outside of Controlled Airspace 91
- Light Signals 92
- Local Procedures 92

Distress and Emergency Calls 93
Priority 94
Distress (MAYDAY) 94
Making a MAYDAY Call 95
Example of a MAYDAY call 95
Urgency (PAN-PAN) 96
Making a PAN-PAN Call 96
Example of a PAN-PAN call 97
Emergency change of level 97
After a MAYDAY or PAN-PAN Radio Call 98
After landing 98
Activation of the ELT 99
Activating the ELT 99
Types of ELT 100
Testing and Inadvertent Activation 100

Examples of Radio Calls 101
Introduction to Making Radio Calls 101
Local Knowledge 101
Category of operation 103
Type of operation 103
Class D No radar CTR Calls – Procedural Aerodrome 105
Example Radio Calls 105
Outbound: Class D no radar CTR Calls – procedural aerodrome 105
Inbound: Class D no radar CTR Calls – procedural aerodrome 105
Operating in the Control Zone: Class D no radar CTR Calls – procedural aerodrome 106
Class D no radar CTA Calls – procedural airspace 107
Outbound: Class D no radar CTA Calls – procedural airspace 107
Inbound: Class D no radar CTA Calls – procedural airspace 108
Class D CTA Calls for IFR flights 109
Outbound: Class D CTA Calls for IFR flights 109
Inbound: Class D CTA Calls for IFR flights 110
Class C Radar Control Zones with separate ACD and Ground 111
Inbound: Class C Radar Control Zones with separate ACD and Ground 111
Outbound: Class C Radar Control Zones with separate ACD and Ground 112
Class G Non-towered aerodrome – CTAF procedures 113
Inbound: Class G Non-towered aerodrome – CTAF procedures 113
Outbound: Class G Non-towered aerodrome – CTAF procedures 113

Radio Waves and Frequencies 114
Radio Waves 114
Mechanical waves 114
Electromagnetic waves 115
Describing electromagnetic energy 115
Amplitude 116
Wavelength and frequency 117
Hertz (Hz) 118
Audio Frequencies 118
Carrier wave 119
Amplitude Modulation (AM) 119
Frequency Modulation (FM) 119
Radio bands 120

       Aviation bands 121
       Low Frequency (LF) and Medium Frequency (MF) 121
       High Frequency (HF) 121
       Very High Frequency (VHF) 121
       Ultra High Frequency (UHF) 122
   Propagation 122
       Direct waves..123
       Sky waves 124
       Ground waves 125
       Reflected waves 125
       Explaining wave interference 126

Know Your Equipment **127**
   Bell206BIII Radio Stack..128
   HeliSAS Autopilot Control Head 129
   Audio Panel 130
   Garmin GPS/NAV/COMM 131
   COMM 2 132
   Automatic Direction Finding (ADF)...132
   Transponder 133
   Traffic Collision Avoidance System (TCAS)...135
   Interfacing with the radios 136
       Headset and helmet 136
       Switches 137
   Summary 139

References **140**

Abbreviations **141**

Aviation Communication and Flight Radio *for Helicopter Pilots*

About this Book

In aviation, where aircraft are moving about in the air at high speeds, being able to communicate effectively with other aircraft, and with people on the ground is vitally important. This book focuses on the knowledge required to communicate using a radio in an aviation environment.

At the foundation of aviation communication, is the conventions for communicating including standard words and phrases, alphabet, numbers, and time. But most importantly, effective communication over the radio relies on how to make a radio call: what to say, how to say it, and when to make a radio call. This book provides a detailed breakdown of radio procedures accompanied by example radio calls. This includes standard radio procedures, distress and emergency calls and what to do when the radio fails.

Essential knowledge about operating a radio in an aviation environment are also explained, including understanding airspace and interpreting maps and charts. This is supported by information about how radio communication works along with descriptions of radio components and equipment.

This book is written in plain English with easy-to-understand explanations supported with many examples, illustrations and photos. While this book follows Australian rules and regulations and provides example radio calls based on operations located in South East Queensland, anyone learning flight radio operations will find this book a valuable resource. It provides a practical easy-to-read guide to aviation communication standards and flight radio operations.

About the Author

Mike Becker is one of Australia's most experienced helicopter instructors, with over 16,000 hours of rotary-wing flight experience. His career has taken him from the mountains in New Zealand to the outback of Australia, to the jungles of Papua New Guinea. He has also worked in the United States, Italy and Borneo.

He has flown a range of helicopter types – the Robinson R22, Robinson R44, Bell 47, Hughes 269, Hughes 500, Bell 206, Bell 427, Bell 212, EC120, Dragon Fly, Brantley B2B, Enstrom EF28, Sikorsky S62A, Hiller

H12ET, Aerospatial AS350, Agusta 109E Power, Agusta 109S Grand, and the Agusta 119 Koala.

He is experienced in a vast range of helicopter operations including high altitude, remote area operations, mustering, firefighting, tourism, sling load operations, specialised long-line operations, search and rescue, and Night Vision Goggles operations.

Mike is a Grade One Flight Instructor and Flight Examiner who holds an Australian Air Transport Pilots Licence (Helicopter) and an Australian Commercial Pilots Licence (Fixed Wing).

Mike is the Chief Pilot and Head of Training for his own business Becker Helicopters in Australia. He, and his wife Jan, established Becker Helicopters in 1997 with one Bell 47 and have grown the business through a love of helicopters, hard work, and determination.

Mike is the recipient of many awards, including the "Captain John Ashton Award for Flight Standards and Aviation Safety" by the Guild of Air Pilots and Air Navigators of London, which was awarded in recognition of over 18,000 accident-free flight training hours at Becker Helicopters. Mike has also authored "Mike Becker's Helicopter Handbook", first published in 1986, along with a range of theory books and instructional videos.

Introduction to Flight Radio

This chapter aims to:

- Introduce the importance of aviation communication, and in particular, radio communications
- Identify factors that help you to communicate
- Identify the factors of an effective radio call
- Describe the basic components of a radio

Importance of Radio Communication

Communication is the key to human interaction.

In aviation, where aircraft are moving about in the air at very high speeds, communicating effectively with other aircraft and people on the ground is vitally important.

The radio is a tool that must be used properly, at the right time, and like anything, requires training and practice.

Figure 1 Atlanta Airport on a normal day (redlegsfan21, 2013)

Factors that help you communicate

Most communication is done face-to-face, with the person you are talking to in front of you.

When communicating face-to-face, other factors help you convey meaning, comprising:

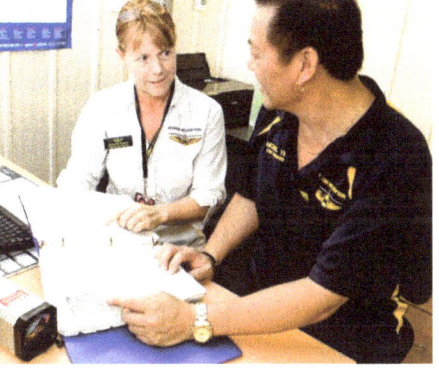

1. **Vocabulary**: That is using words that have particular meaning to what we are trying to communicate.
2. **Vocal pitch** of the voice when speaking the words, comprising:
   (a) **Pitch**: high squeaky voice or low deep voice
   (b) **Speed**: the rate at which the words are spoken
   (c) **Volume**: how loud or quiet the words are spoken, and
   (d) **Tone**: how they are spoken, for example, happy, sad, angry, or normal.
3. **Body language**, including facial expressions, eye contact, hand and other gestures.

Face-to-face vs radio communication

Universal facial expressions

There are seven (7) universal facial expressions as follows:

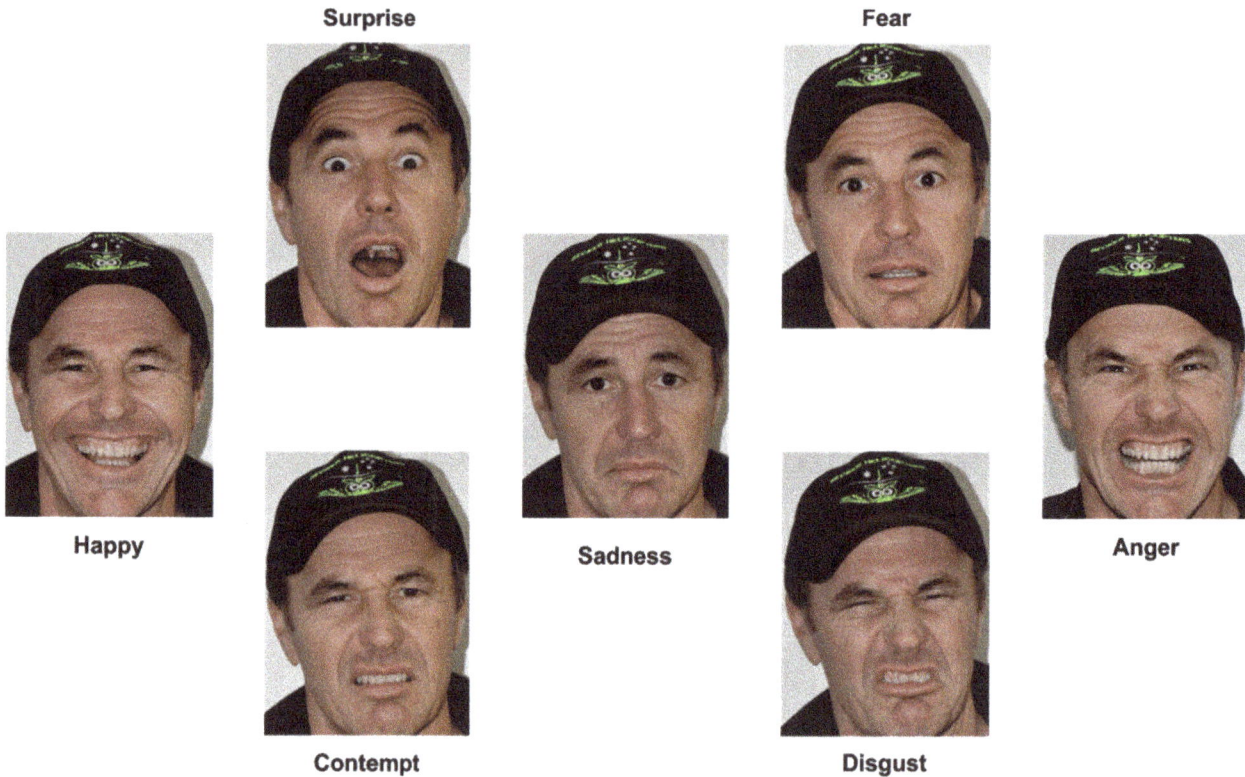

Interestingly, in face-to-face communication, only **7%** of our effective communication comes from spoken words, the other **55%** is through body language, and **38%** is through the vocal pitch.

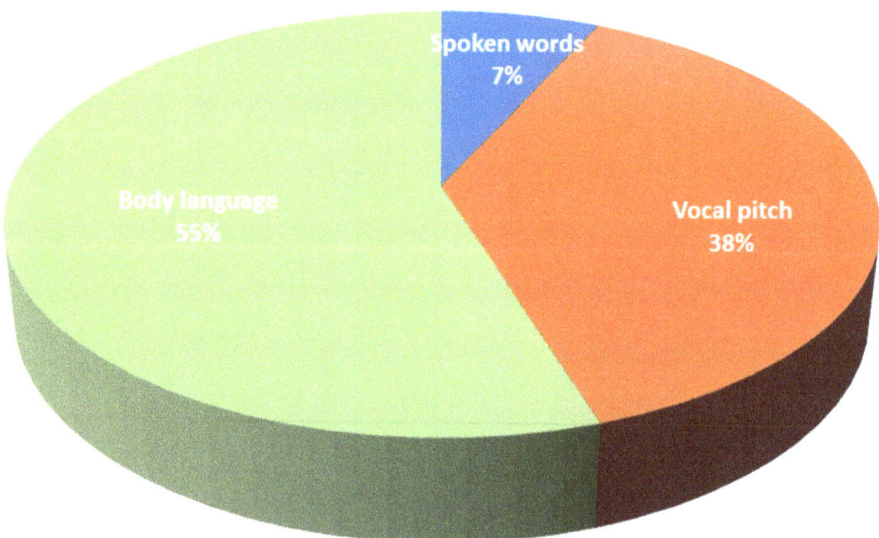

Therefore, when talking on the radio, we lose almost 93% of our main communication tools compared to communicating face-to-face. This means communicating on the radio can be difficult as we rely on only **7%** of our communication tools to fully understand what the other person is saying.

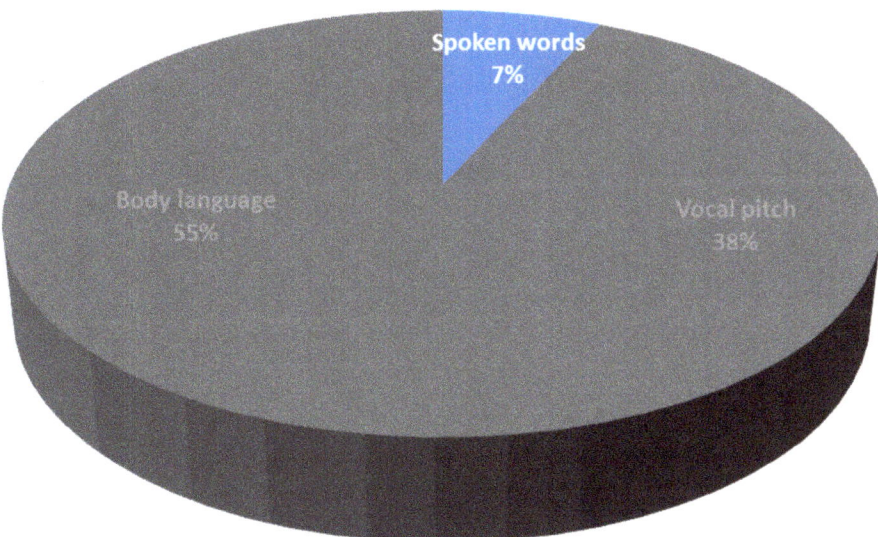

Using the correct vocabulary becomes vitally important.

When communicating on the radio you must be aware that whatever you **SAY** is what the other person will **BELIEVE,** even if it is not what you **MEAN**.

To have an effective radio call, both the sender and the receiver must be using the same communication tools and be using the same standard words.

Elements of An Effective Radio Call

An effective radio call has four (4) elements. It is:

- Clear
- Concise
- Consistent, and
- Correct.

Clear

When making a radio call, others must be able to clearly hear and understand what you are saying. You need to speak directly into the microphone using standard phraseology slightly slower than you would typically use in everyday conversation. Remember the receiving person cannot see you, so:

- they cannot see your gestures or posture,
- they may not be able to hear the tone of your voice, so
- what you say needs to be specific.

Concise

Concise means that radio calls should be short and to the point. Give the relevant information only.

Consistent

Consistent means that radio calls should follow a similar or consistent pattern. If using standard phraseology in the same order, you are more likely to get your message across.

Correct

Most importantly, you need to be accurate. Whatever you say, the receiving party will believe, so it is important to get it right. This is most relevant when stating your position, height and intentions.

Mike Becker, Becker Helicopters

What is radio?

To better understand the radio, let's run through some basic radio theory before moving on to how to use the radio in the aviation environment.

Radio is the wireless transmission (radiation) of electromagnetic signals through the atmosphere or space. Attached to these electromagnetic signals is sound or images, which can then be extracted from the electromagnetic signals and listened to or viewed.

History

During the late 1800s, several physicists predicted the existence of radio waves, but in 1886 a German physicist, Heinrich Hertz, demonstrated that rapid variations of electric current could be projected into space in the form of radio waves like those of light and heat.

In 1895, Gugliemo Marconi sent and received the first radio signal in Italy. By 1899 he flashed the first wireless signal across the English Channel, and in 1902 received the letter "S", telegraphed from England to Newfoundland, the first successful transatlantic radiotelegraph message.

From this point on, the use of radio and its development continued to what we have today.

Components

To make and receive a radio transmission requires several different components.

The pilot first speaks into a microphone (electrical transducer) to make a radio call, which converts the sound into an electrical signal that travels via wires to a radio box. This radio box has electronic processors and a transmitter that sends out an electromagnetic wave via an antenna that has been modulated (or changed) to carry the signal.

The electromagnetic wave is intercepted by another antenna that channels it to a receiver. A receiver is another radio box with electronic processors that translates the electromagnetic signal and extracts the original electrical signal. This signal travels by wires to the earphones (another electrical transducer) that converts the electrical signal back to sound that we can hear and understand.

Therefore, most radios have both a transmitter and a receiver so 2-way communication is possible.

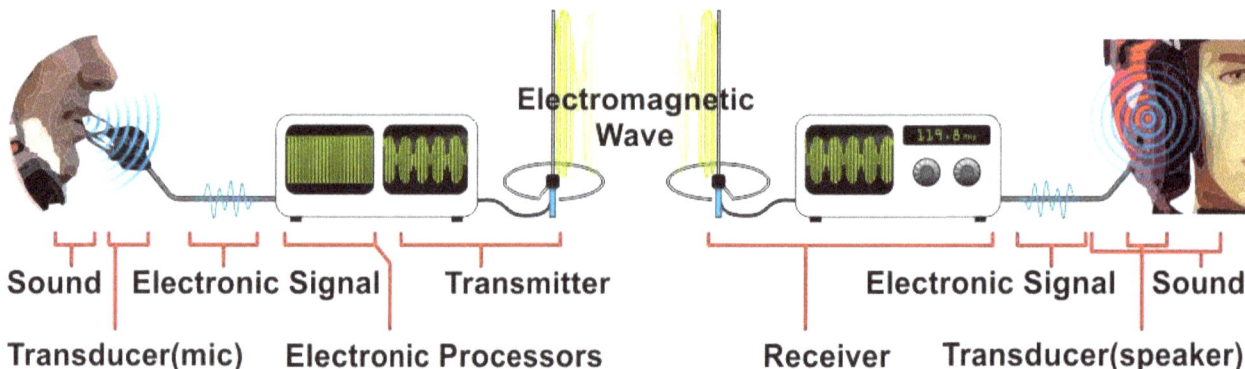

Aviation Communication and Flight Radio *for Helicopter Pilots*

Components of a Radio

Radio consists of the following major components:

1. Microphone
2. Wiring
3. Transmitter and Receiver
4. Antenna, and
5. Speaker.

1 — Microphone

A microphone converts the original sound into electricity (called a transducer in electronic terms).

2 — Wiring

Wiring, cables, connections and terminals allow the electrical signal to travel to and from the radio box and the various components. There can be miles of wiring running between the various components in an aircraft. Some of this wiring in modern aircraft is being replaced by wireless and Bluetooth technology.

3 — Transmitter and receiver

A radio box has electronic processors in it that allows the unit to be:

- a transmitter, or
- a receiver, or
- both (called a transceiver).

For example, inside the Bendix/King VHF radio box.

Both the transmitter and the receiver will have the same basic components, including:

- a power supply
- an oscillator to generate a radio frequency carrier wave and control the frequency of the signal generated
- an amplifier to increase the output energy of the signal
- a modulator that is responsible for giving intelligence to the signal, where it codes for the transmitter and decodes for the receiver.

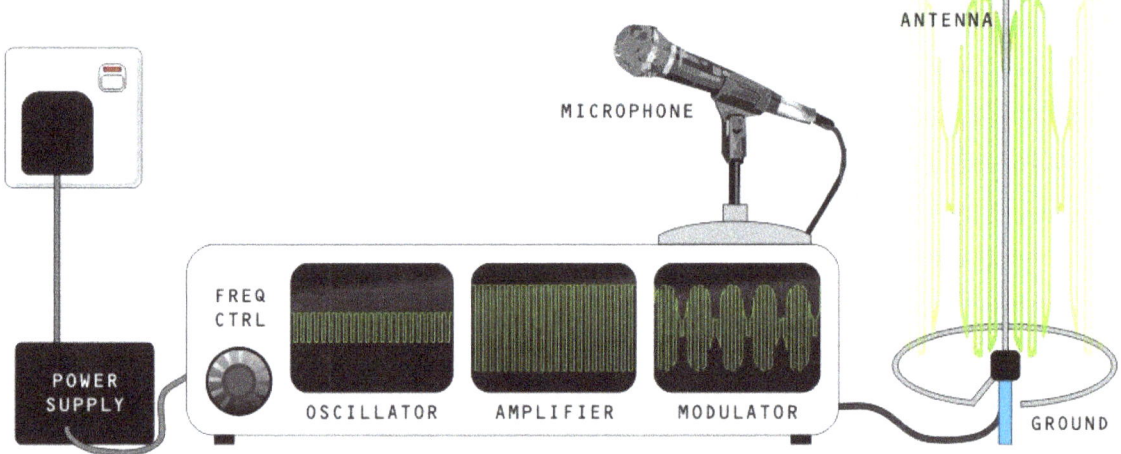

Scanner

A radio box that only has a receiver is called a "Scanner" or "Receiver" as it only accepts signals; it cannot transmit them.

Transceiver

A radio box that can both receive and transmit signals is called a "Transceiver", which is what is installed in aircraft.

4 — Antenna

The antenna projects an electromagnetic wave that carries the embedded signal from the radio box. It also receives an incoming electromagnetic wave and sends it to the radio box for decoding.

5 — Speaker

A speaker (usually installed in a set of earphones as part of a headset or helmet) translates the electrical signal back into sound that we can understand (a transducer in electronic terms).

Flight Radio Operator Rules

Aim

This chapter aims to:

- Make the trainee aware of the Australian regulations related to aviation communication and operating a radio in an aircraft.

Introduction

Most rules and regulations around the operation of radio in aviation are based on information from the International Civil Aviation Organisation (ICAO).

A trainee must have a good level of English before commencing flying training. Without English skills, it is difficult to be understood and to understand what is said on the radio.

ICAO English levels

A pilot is required by international law to speak and understand English to operate an aircraft radio. As pilots come from different countries and speak different languages, levels of English skills vary.

ICAO has defined six (6) skill levels of Aviation English. The competencies required for Aviation English are defined for each level. Further, each level specifies any requirements to regularly re-test the individual to ensure a continued English level.

The ICAO Aviation English levels of skill are described below.

Level 6: Expert

Pronunciation

Pronunciation, stress, rhythm, and intonation, though possibly influenced by the first language or regional variation, almost never interfere with ease of understanding.

Structure

Both basic and complex grammatical structures and sentence patterns are consistently well controlled.

Vocabulary

Vocabulary range and accuracy are sufficient to communicate effectively on a wide variety of familiar and unfamiliar topics. Vocabulary is idiomatic, nuanced, and sensitive to register.

Fluency

Able to speak at length with a natural, effortless flow. Varies speech flow for stylistic effect, for example, to emphasise a point. Uses appropriate discourse markers and connectors spontaneously.

Comprehension

Comprehension is consistently accurate in nearly all contexts and includes comprehension of linguistic and cultural subtleties.

Interactions

Interacts with ease in nearly all situations. Is sensitive to verbal and non-verbal cues and responds to them appropriately.

Level 5: Extended

Pronunciation

Pronunciation, stress, rhythm, and intonation, though influenced by the first language or regional variation, rarely interfere with ease of understanding.

Structure

Basic grammatical structures and sentence patterns are consistently well controlled. Complex structures are attempted but with errors that sometimes interfere with meaning.

Vocabulary

Vocabulary range and accuracy are sufficient to communicate effectively on common, concrete, and work-related topics. Paraphrases consistently and successfully. Vocabulary is sometimes idiomatic.

Fluency

Able to speak at length with relative ease on familiar topics but may not vary speech flow as a stylistic device. Can make use of appropriate discourse markers or connectors.

Comprehension

Able to speak at length with relative ease on familiar topics but may not vary speech flow as a stylistic device. Can make use of appropriate discourse markers or connectors.

Interactions

Responses are immediate, appropriate, and informative. Manages the speaker/listener relationship effectively.

Level 4: Operational

Pronunciation

Pronunciation, stress, rhythm, and intonation are influenced by the first language or regional variation but only sometimes interfere with ease of understanding.

Structure

Basic grammatical structures and sentence patterns are used creatively and are usually well controlled. Errors may occur, particularly in unusual or unexpected circumstances, but rarely interfere with meaning.

Vocabulary

Vocabulary range and accuracy are usually sufficient to communicate effectively on common, concrete, and work-related topics. Can often paraphrase successfully when lacking vocabulary in unusual or unexpected circumstances.

Fluency

Produces stretches of language at an appropriate tempo. There may be occasional loss of fluency on transition from rehearsed or formulaic speech to spontaneous interaction, but this does not prevent effective communication. Can make limited use of discourse markers or connectors. Fillers are not distracting.

Comprehension

Produces stretches of language at an appropriate tempo. There may be occasional loss of fluency on transition from rehearsed or formulaic speech to spontaneous interaction, but this does not prevent effective communication. Can make limited use of discourse markers or connectors. Fillers are not distracting.

Interactions

Responses are usually immediate, appropriate, and informative. Initiates and maintains exchanges even when dealing with an unexpected turn of events. Deals adequately with apparent misunderstandings by checking, confirming, or clarifying.

Level 3: Pre-Operational

Pronunciation

Pronunciation, stress, rhythm, and intonation are influenced by the first language or regional variation and frequently interfere with ease of understanding.

Structure

Basic grammatical structures and sentence patterns associated with predictable situations are not always well controlled. Errors frequently interfere with meaning.

Vocabulary

Vocabulary range and accuracy are often sufficient to communicate on common, concrete, or work-related topics, but the range is limited and the word choice is often inappropriate. Is often unable to paraphrase successfully when lacking vocabulary.

Fluency

Produces stretches of language, but the phrasing and pausing are often inappropriate. Hesitations or slowness in language processing may prevent effective communication. Fillers are sometimes distracting.

Comprehension

Comprehension is often accurate on common, concrete and work-related topics when the accent or variety used is sufficiently intelligible for an international community of users. May fail to understand a linguistic or situational complication or an unexpected turn of events.

Interactions

Responses are sometimes immediate, appropriate, and informative. Can initiate and maintain exchanges with reasonable ease on familiar topics and in predictable situations. Generally inadequate when dealing with an unexpected turn of events.

Level 2: Elementary

Pronunciation

Pronunciation, stress, rhythm, and intonation are heavily influenced by the first language or regional variation and usually interfere with ease of understanding.

Structure

Shows only limited control of a few simple memorised grammatical structures and sentence patterns.

Vocabulary

Limited vocabulary range consisting only of isolated words and memorised phrases.

Fluency

Can produce very short, isolated, memorised utterances with frequent pausing and distracting use of fillers to search for expressions and to articulate less familiar words.

Comprehension

Comprehension is limited to isolated, memorised phrases when they are carefully and slowly articulated.

Interactions

Response time is slow and often inappropriate. Interaction is limited to simple routine exchanges.

Level 1: Pre-Elementary

Performs at a level below the Elementary level.

Aviation Communication and Flight Radio *for Helicopter Pilots*

Flight Radio Operator Rules in Australia

In Australia, student pilots are only allowed to use the radio when under the supervision of an instructor.

To gain a Flight Radio Operator qualification, the trainee must:

- hold a minimum of ICAO Level 4 in English
- have completed a Flight Radio Operators Licence (FROL) course
- have been assessed as competent in using the radio by an instructor.

What does a FROL allow you to do

On completing a FROL, the user can operate aircraft radio systems for aviation communication.

Relevant documents

The following is a list of the relevant CASR Part 61 sections related to Flight Radio for trainees and Pilots that you may need to reference when asked.

- Part 61.120 Operation of an aircraft without a licence
- Part 61.435 When holders of pilot licenses' authorised to operate aircraft radio
- Part 61.1227 Obligations of pilot instructors – approval to operate aircraft radio
- Part 61.255 English Language Proficiency
- Part 61.250 Duration of English Language Proficiency Assessments
- Part 61.260 Duration of English Language Proficiency Assessments
- Part 61.270 Approval of English Language Assessors
- Part 61.275 Overseas Flight Crew Authorisations – recognition
- Part 61.1225 Obligations of Pilot Instructors
- Part 61 Manual of Standards (MOS) Section 2: Language Proficiency

Training Course

A Flight Radio Operators License (FROL) course is a requirement to obtain the FROL. Training typically consists of a theory portion, some practice on the ground and in the aircraft with the instructor, followed by a written and then a practical assessment.

In real terms, much of this happens as a normal part of the trainees flying activities whilst receiving instruction during the course.

Assessment

The assessment includes normal and abnormal use of the radio and a clear demonstration to the instructor that you can speak and understand English on the radio so that the helicopter can be operated safely in and around airports and other aircraft.

To be an operational pilot at the Commercial level, an individual shall have as a minimum an **ICAO level 4** in English. Different levels of ICAO Aviation English require a pilot to be re-tested periodically, as detailed in the table below.

ICAO Level	Testing required
6	No re-testing is required.
5	Every 6 years.
4	Every 3 years.

Competency scale

The following extract is taken from the CASA Part 61 Manual of Standards (MOS) and describes the competency levels required to achieve an ICAO level 4, 5 or 6 in Australia.

Applicability

The following rating scale applies to Aviation English language proficiency assessments:

- Level 6 – expert level
- Level 5 – extended
- Level 4 – operational.

Requirements

A Trainee or Pilot is required to comprehend (understand) English within the six (6) categories (Pronunciation, Structure, Vocabulary, Fluency, Comprehension and Interactions) as shown and described in the previous table to be assessed as competent within the associated ICAO English Levels 1 thru to 6.

Below are the expanded rating requirements for levels 4, 5 and 6. Achieving one of these levels is required for a Commercial Pilot.

Aviation Communication and Flight Radio *for Helicopter Pilots*

Rating scale

Level 6 - Expert

- The person must communicate effectively face to face using clear and precise English so that each of the following is the case for the person:
    - pronunciation, stress, rhythm and intonation, though possibly influenced by the first language or regional variation, almost never interfere with ease of understanding;
    - both basic and complex grammatical structures and sentence patterns are consistently well controlled;
    - vocabulary range and accuracy are sufficient to communicate effectively on a wide variety of familiar and unfamiliar topics;
    - vocabulary is idiomatic, nuanced and sensitive to register;
    - able to speak at length with a natural, effortless flow;
    - varies speech flow for stylistic effect, e.g. to emphasise a point;
    - uses appropriate discourse markers and connectors spontaneously;
    - comprehension is consistently accurate in nearly all contexts and includes comprehension of linguistic and cultural subtleties;
    - interacts with ease in nearly all situations;
    - is sensitive to verbal and non-verbal cues and responds to them appropriately
- The person communicates effectively in voice-only radio/telephone communication using standard aviation phraseology so that each of the following is the case for the person:
    - makes appropriate transmissions using standard aviation phraseology;
    - uses plain English effectively when standard phraseology is inadequate;
    - receives appropriate responses to transmissions;
    - responds to transmissions and takes appropriate action;
    - identifies and manages communication errors and misunderstandings promptly and effectively;
    - seeks clarification in the time available if the message is unclear or if there is uncertainty about the message;
    - reacts appropriately to a variety of regional accents;
    - communicates effectively in unexpected, stressful or non-standard situations using standard phraseology or plain English.

Level 5 – Extended

- The person must communicate effectively face to face using clear and precise English so that each of the following is the case for the person:
    - stress, rhythm and intonation, though influenced by the first language or regional variation, rarely interfere with ease of understanding;
    - basic grammatical structures and sentence patterns are consistently well controlled. Complex structures are attempted but with errors that sometimes interfere with meaning;
    - vocabulary range and accuracy are sufficient to communicate effectively on common, concrete, and work-related topics. Para-phrases consistently and successfully. Vocabulary is sometimes idiomatic;
    - able to speak at length with relative ease on familiar topics but may not vary speech flow as a stylistic device. Can make use of appropriate discourse markers or connectors;
    - comprehension is accurate on common, concrete, and work-related topics and mostly accurate when the speaker is confronted with a linguistic or situational complication or an unexpected turn of events. Can comprehend a range of speech varieties (dialect and/ accent) or registers;
    - interacts with ease in nearly all situations. Is sensitive to verbal and non-verbal cues and responds to them appropriately;
    - responses are usually immediate, appropriate and informative. Initiates and maintains exchanges even when dealing with an unexpected turn of events. Deals adequately with apparent misunderstandings by checking, confirming or clarifying.
- The person must communicate effectively in voice-only radio/telephone communication using standard aviation phraseology so that each of the following is the case for the person:

- makes appropriate transmissions using standard aviation phraseology;
- uses plain English effectively when standard phraseology is inadequate;
- receives appropriate responses to transmissions;
- responds to transmissions and takes appropriate action;
- identifies and manages communication errors and/or misunderstandings promptly and effectively;
- seeks clarification in the time available if a message is unclear or uncertainty exists;
- reacts appropriately to a variety of regional accents;
- communicates effectively in unexpected, stressful or non-standard situations using standard phraseology or plain English.

Level 4 – Operational

- The person must communicate effectively face to face using clear and precise English so that each of the following is the case for the person:
    - Stress, rhythm and intonation are influenced by the first language or regional variation but only sometimes interfere with ease of understanding;
    - Basic grammatical structures and sentence patterns are used creatively and are usually well controlled. Errors may occur, particularly in unusual or unexpected circumstances, but rarely interfere with meaning;
    - Vocabulary range and accuracy are usually sufficient to communicate effectively on common, concrete, and work-related topics. Can often paraphrase successfully when lacking vocabulary in unusual or unexpected circumstances;
    - Produces stretches of language at an appropriate tempo. There may be occasional loss of fluency on transition from rehearsed or formulaic speech to spontaneous interaction, but this does not prevent effective communication. Can make limited use of discourse markers or connectors. Fillers are not distracting;
    - Comprehension is mostly accurate on common, concrete and work-related topics when the accent or variety used is sufficiently intelligible for an international community of users. When the speaker is confronted with a linguistic or situational complication or an unexpected turn of events, comprehension may be slower or require clarification strategies;
    - Responses are usually immediate, appropriate and informative. Initiates and maintains exchanges even when dealing with an unexpected turn of events. Deals adequately with apparent misunderstandings by checking, confirming or clarifying.
- The person communicates effectively in voice-only radio/telephone communication using standard aviation phraseology so that each of the following is the case for the person:
    - makes appropriate transmissions using standard aviation phraseology;
    - uses plain English effectively when standard phraseology is inadequate;
    - receives appropriate responses to transmissions;
    - responds to transmissions and takes appropriate action;
    - identifies and manages communication errors and/or misunderstandings promptly and effectively;
    - seeks clarification in the time available if a message is unclear or uncertainty exists;
    - reacts appropriately to a variety of regional accents;
    - Communicates effectively in unexpected, stressful or non-standard situations using standard phraseology or plain English.

Aviation Communication and Flight Radio *for Helicopter Pilots*

Standard Words and Phrases

This chapter aims to review the aviation standards for:

- letters and numbers
- phrases and words
- commonly used abbreviations; and
- writing words in shorthand.

Introduction to Standard Words and Phrases

To easily understand each other, the use of standard words, phrases and the way we pronounce these words and phrases is important. This is particularly essential in a helicopter environment, where it is often hard to hear due to excessive noise. This does not mean that you cannot use common language if it is required to be understood, but it does mean that your radio calls must be clear and concise and, where possible, use standard phraseology.

Remember, what you think you understand may not be what is meant. Standard words and phrases help fix this, ensuring a common understanding of aviation terms and phrases.

What the Trainee hears

OK Mohammed blah blah blah blah, blah blah blah blah blah blah blah ERSA blah blah blah blah blah blah blah blah blah blah blah VHF radio blah blah .blah blah blah blah blah blah ground blah blah blah blblah blah ah ATIS blah blah blah blah run-up blah blah blah blah blah, understand?

What the instructor says

OK Mohammed what I want you to do is find the radio frequency in the ERSA and then dial up the frequency on the primary VHF radio. Once you have done that I want you to transmit to the ground and tell them exactly what you want to do, but you have to get the ATIS first and run through all the run-up procedures, do you understand?

Phonetic Alphabet

The phonetic alphabet assigns a word to each letter and describes how each word is to be pronounced.

No	Word	Phonetic
A	Alpha	AL fah
B	Bravo	BRAH VOH
C	Charlie	CHAR lee
D	Delta	DELL tah
E	Echo	ECK oh
F	Foxtrot	FOKS trot
G	Golf	golf
H	Hotel	Hoh TELL
I	India	IN dee ah
J	Juliet	JEW lee ETT
K	Kilo	KEY loh
L	Lima	LEE mah
M	Mike	Mike
N	November	No VEM ber
O	Oscar	OSS car
P	Papa	Pah PAH
Q	Quebec	Key BECK
R	Romeo	ROW me oh
S	Sierra	See AIR ah
T	Tango	TANG go
U	Uniform	YOU nee form
V	Victor	VICK tah
W	Whiskey	WISS key
X	Xray	ECKS ray
Y	Yankee	YANK key
Z	Zulu	ZOO loo

Numbers

There is a standardised way to pronounce each number to ensure clarity when communicating numbers over the radio.

No	Word	Phonetic
0	Zero	ZE-RO
1	One	WUN
2	Two	TOO
3	Three	THREE (or TREE)
4	Four	FOWer
5	Five	FIFE
6	Six	SIX
7	Seven	SEVen
8	Eight	AIT
9	Nine	NINer
.	Decimal	DAY SEE MAL
100	Hundred	HUNdred
1000	Thousand	THOUSAND (or TOU-SAND)
50	Five zero	FIFE ZE-RO
85	Eight five	AIT FIFE
612	Six One Two	SIX WUN TOO
900	Nine Hundred	NINer HUNdred
3,000	Three Thousand	TREE TOU-SAND
3,500	Three Thousand five hundred	TREE TOU-SAND FIFE HUNdred
12,000	One two thousand	WUN TOO TOU-SAND
12,700	One two thousand seven hundred	WUN TOO TOU-SAND SEVen HUNdred
12,755	One two seven five five	WUN TOO SEVen FIFE FIFE
118.3	One one eight decimal three	WUN WUN AIT DAY-SEE-MAL TREE

Measurements

Vertical Measurements (Height)

Vertical measurements such as altitude (for aircraft or cloud) are in feet, where one foot equals approximately 30cm.

Altitude (Feet)

Number	Spoken
800	Eight Hundred
1,500	One thousand five hundred

Cloud Height (Feet)

Number	Spoken
2,200	Two thousand two hundred
4,300	Four thousand three hundred

Horizontal Measurements (Visibility - Distance)

Horizontal measurements for visibility or cloud separation are in metres or kilometres.

Visibility (meters)

Number	Spoken
200 m	Two hundred
3,000 m	Three thousand

Visibility (Kilometres)

Number	Spoken
8 km	Eight kilometres

Horizontal Measurements (Distances)

In Australia, we use nautical miles for calculating distance. One nautical mile is the same as 1.85 km.

Distance for Navigation (nautical miles)

Number	Spoken
2 nm	Two nautical miles
15 nm	One five nautical miles

Speed

Airspeed is measured in knots, where one knot is equal to one nautical mile per hour (one KT = one NM/H).

Aircraft Speed (Knots)

Number	Spoken
100 kt	One hundred knots

Headings and Direction

Headings are measured in degrees, related to the magnetic compass and are always spoken as three individual digits. The wind's direction also uses the same three-digit format followed by two digits for the wind strength in knots.

Heading (degrees)

Number	Spoken
150	One five zero
080	Zero eight zero

Wind Speeds (knots)

Number	Spoken
70 kt	Seven zero knots
18 kt gusting 30	One eight knots gusting three zero

Mike Becker, Becker Helicopters

Time in Aviation

Aircraft often move between time zones. Aviation uses a specific time reference known as **coordinated universal time** (UTC), which is the same as Greenwich mean time (GMT). The code letter for this time zone is Z (Zulu). The 24-hour clock system is used to convey time.

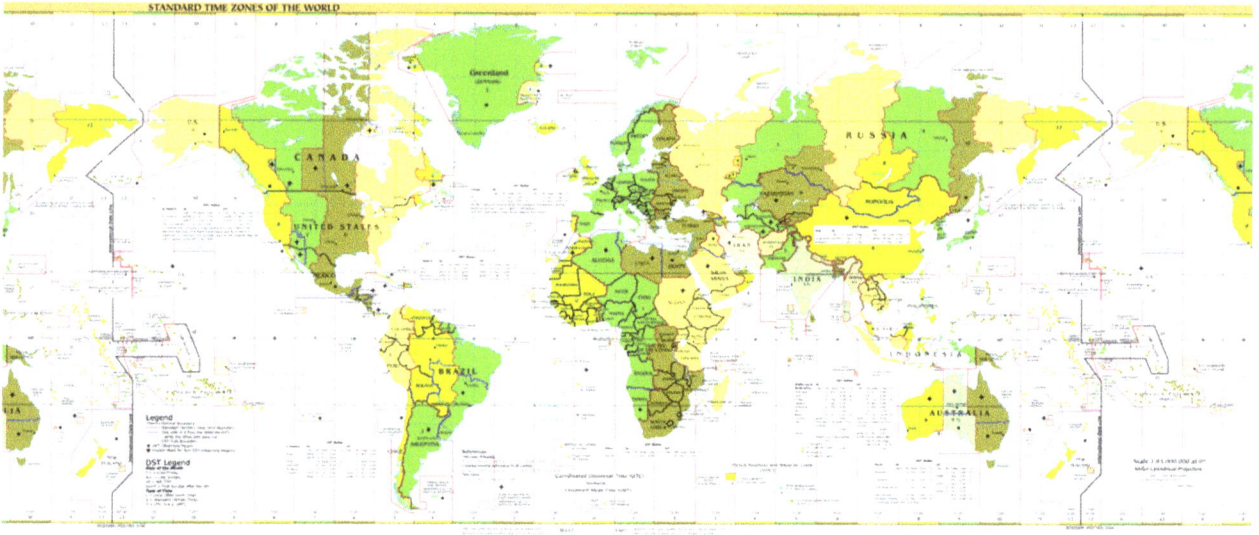

Local Time

Local time is often given a name, for example, Eastern Time. Local time may be represented by how many hours ahead or behind that location is from UTC. For example, Eastern Time in the USA may be referred to as UTC -5, while Brisbane is UTC+10.

Daylight Saving Time

Times zones may apply Daylight Saving Time (DST), usually during the summer months. This time is also given a name, for example, Eastern Time becomes Eastern Daylight Time during daylight saving time.

Local Time in the USA

The US has six time zones illustrated in the diagram below, plus additional time zones for dependencies and territories.

Aviation Communication and Flight Radio *for Helicopter Pilots*

Time Zones in the US

Abbreviation	Time Zone Name	UTC offset	Example City
HST	Hawaii Standard Time	-10	Honolulu
AKST	Alaska Standard Time	-9	Anchorage
PST	Pacific Standard Time	-8	Los Angeles
MST	Mountain Standard Time	-7	Salt Lake City
CST	Central Standard Time	-6	Chicago
EST	Eastern Standard Time	-5	New York

Daylight savings time in the US

Abbreviation	Time Zone Name	UTC offset	Example City
HDT	Hawaii Daylight Time	-9	Honolulu
AKDT	Alaska Daylight Time	-8	Anchorage
PDT	Pacific Daylight Time	-7	Los Angeles
MDT	Mountain Daylight Time	-6	Salt Lake City
CDT	Central Daylight Time	-5	Chicago
EDT	Eastern Daylight Time	-4	New York

Local Time in Australia

The diagram below summarises the Australian time zones.

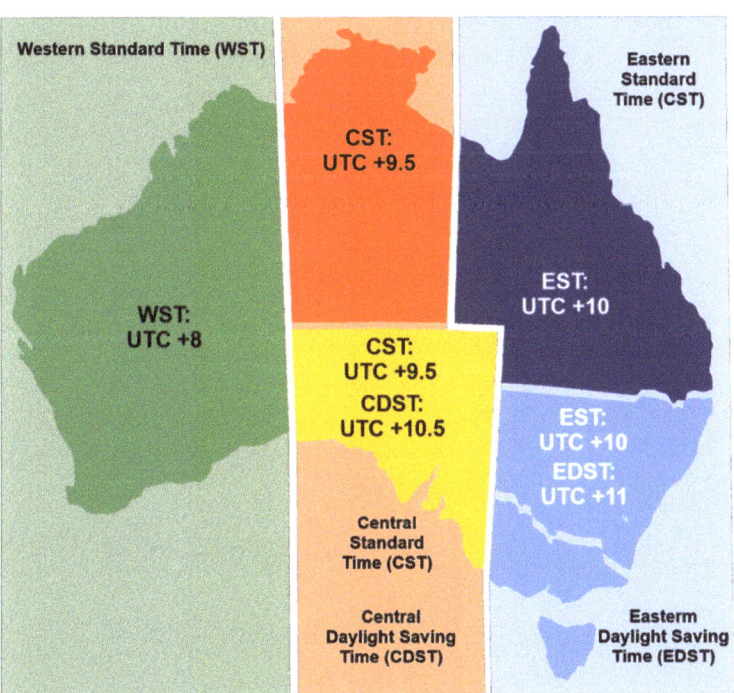

Australia falls into three separate time zones:

Abbreviation	Time Zone Name	UTC offset	States
EST	Eastern Standard Time	+10	NSW, QLD, VIC, ACT and TAS
CST	Central Standard Time	+9.5	SA and NT
WST	Western Standard Time	+8	WA

Daylight Savings Time in Australia

Daylight saving is not applied universally across Australia. QLD, NT and WA do not have daylight savings. When daylight savings apply, the following time zones apply:

Abbreviation	Time Zone Name	UTC offset	States
EDST	Eastern Daylight Savings Time	+11	NSW, VIC, ACT and TAS. *Not QLD*
CDST	Central Daylight Savings Time	+10.5	SA. *Not WA*

Transmitting Time

When transmitting time, pilots quote time to the **nearest minute**, excluding the hour.

Transmit the time in full if:

- the time occurs in a different hour, or
- there is any possibility of misunderstanding.

Examples

Time	Transmitted as	Alternatively
0815	One five	Zero eight one five
1720	Two zero	One seven two zero
2300	Two three zero zero	Two three zero zero zulu
0400	Zero four zero zero	

Air Traffic Control

While pilots quote time to the nearest minute, Air Traffic Control quote time to the **nearest minute or half-minute**.

Examples

Time	Transmitted as
0925:10	Time two five
0932:20	Time Three Two and a Half
2145:50	Time Four Six

Standard Words and Phrases

The following words and phrases have been standardised for aviation radio communication with a defined meaning:

ACKNOWLEDGE

"Let me know that you have received and understood this message."

AFFIRMATIVE

"Yes." (sometimes abbreviated to AFIRM)

APPROVED

"Permission for proposed action granted."

BREAK

"I hereby indicate the separation between portions of the message." (To be used where there is no clear distinction between the text and other portions of the message.)

BREAK BREAK

"I hereby indicate the separation between messages transmitted to different aircraft in a very busy environment."

CANCEL

"Annul the previously transmitted clearance."

CHECK

"Examine a system or procedure." (Not to be used in any other context. No answer is normally expected.)

CLEARED

"Authorised to proceed under the conditions specified."

CONFIRM

"I request verification of: (clearance, instruction, action, information)."

CONTACT

"Establish communication with..."

CORRECT

"True" or "Accurate".

CORRECTION

"An error has been made in this transmission (or message indicated). The correct version is..."

DISREGARD

"Ignore."

GO AHEAD

"Proceed with your message." Note: Not used whenever the possibility exists of misconstruing "GO AHEAD" as an authorisation for an aircraft to proceed. The phrase "GO AHEAD" may be omitted and, in its place, a response made by using the calling aeronautical station's callsign followed by the answering aeronautical station's callsign.

HOW DO YOU READ

"What is the readability of my transmission?"

I SAY AGAIN

"I repeat for clarity or emphasis."

MAINTAIN

"Continue in accordance with the condition(s) specified" or in its literal sense, e.g. "Maintain VFR".

MONITOR

"Listen out on (frequency)."

NEGATIVE

"No" or "Permission not granted" or "That is not correct" or "Not capable".

OVER

"My transmission is ended, and I expect a response from you." Note: Not normally used in VHF communication.

OUT

"This exchange of transmissions is ended and no response is expected." Note: Not normally used in VHF communication.

READ BACK

"Repeat all, or the specified part, of this message back to me exactly as received."

RECLEARED

"A change has been made to your last clearance and this new clearance supersedes your previous clearance or part thereof."

REPORT

"Pass me the following information..."

REQUEST

"I should like to know..." or "I wish to obtain..."

ROGER

"I have received all of your last transmission." Note: Under no circumstances to be used in reply to a question requiring "READ BACK" or a direct answer in the affirmative (AFFIRM) or negative (NEGATIVE).

SAY AGAIN

"Repeat all, or the following part, of your last transmission."

SPEAK SLOWER

"Reduce your rate of speech."

STANDBY

"Wait and I will call you." Note: The caller would normally re-establish contact if the delay is lengthy. STANDBY is not an approval or denial.

UNABLE

"I cannot comply with your request, instruction, or clearance." Note: UNABLE is normally followed by a reason.

WILCO

(Abbreviation for "will comply".) "I understand your message and will comply with it."

WORDS TWICE

(1) As a request: "Communication is difficult. Please send every word, or group of words, twice."

(2) As information: "Since communication is difficult, every word, or group of words, in this message will be sent twice."

… Aviation Communication and Flight Radio *for Helicopter Pilots*

Abbreviations, Acronym, and Mnemonics

Keeping what you say short and to the point in radio communications is very important. Therefore, we use abbreviations, acronyms and mnemonics to keep our radio calls short as well as to help us remember essential flight procedures.

Abbreviations (Abb)

Abbreviates are the shortened form of words or phrases used frequently. For example, you can abbreviate names.

Mike	Michael
Tim	Timothy
Bev	Beverley

Aviation terms used all the time:

TWR	Tower
ACFT	Aircraft
ARR	Arrive / Arrival

Units of measurement are also often shortened:

Hr	Hour
Min	Minutes
Km	Kilometres
KT	Knots

Other words or expressions are also abbreviated:

OK	Okay
Auto	Automatic
Wilco	Will comply
Max	Maximum

Method of Abbreviation

There are different methods to create abbreviations.

- Taking out the vowels, for example:
    - TWR = Tower
    - CLR = Clear
- Using the first letters, for example:
    - VIS = Visibility
    - ARR = Arrival
    - DEP = Departure

There are no fixed rules for making abbreviations.

City Names and Airport Codes

The International Civil Aviation Organisation (ICAO: this is an acronym but more on those later) has given each airport around the world its own abbreviation/code to make it easy to identify an airport and the country where the airport is located. The table below provides two examples:

	Switzerland	**Australia**
Initial Letter	LS	Y
	Bern Airport	**Brisbane Airport**
ICAO Code	LSZB	YBBN
FAA Code	BRN	BNE
	Zurich Airport	**Melbourne Airport**
ICAO Code	LSZH	YMML
FAA Code	WRH	MEL

The ICAO code is the code used in aviation, while the Federal Aviation Administration (FAA) code is the code used within the airport for things like passenger tickets and baggage stamps. If you have ever flown to another country, you would have seen the FAA code on your ticket and the departures board, which tells you what gate to go to for your flight.

Acronyms

Acronyms are words formed using the first letters of a word or phrase.

You have already come across acronyms such as ICAO and FAA.

Acronym	Meaning
MTOW	**M**aximum **T**ake-**o**ff **W**eight
MSL	**M**ean **S**ea **L**evel
AMSL	**A**bove **M**ean **S**ea **L**evel
POB	**P**ersons **o**n **B**oard
ROD	**R**ate **o**f **D**escent
WAC	**W**orld **A**eronautical **C**hart
ASAP	**A**s **s**oon **as** **p**ossible

Mnemonics

There is a lot to remember in aviation, so we use mnemonics to make it easier to remember things in a specific order. You would have probably already used some of these at school.

- **Roy G Biv** [colours of rainbow]
- **My Very Elegant Mother Just Served Us Nine Pizzas** [the nine planets]
- **HEFFR** [helicopter pre-takeoff checklist]
- **PSWAT** [helicopter landing pad checklist]

Roy G Biv is a mnemonic used for remembering the order of the colours of the rainbow:

R	Red
O	Orange
Y	Yellow
G	Green
B	Blue
I	Indigo
V	Violet

(This mnemonic is also an acronym)

My Very Elegant Mother Just Served Us Nine Pizzas is a good way of remembering the order of the nine planets.

My	Mercury
Very	Venus
Elegant	Earth
Mother	Mars
Just	Jupiter
Served	Saturn
Us	Uranus
Nine	Neptune
Pizzas	Pluto

We also use many mnemonics to help us remember the order of flight procedures, for example, the HEFFR pre-takeoff check and the PSWAT approaching landing site checks.

HEFFR pre-takeoff check

H	Hatches, harness, homework & helipad
E	Engine and instruments. Warning lights out, governor ON, instruments set
F	Fuel: calculate time in the air and convert to time on a watch
F	Frictions off
R	Radio and radiation

PSWAT checks for approaching a landing site

P	Power, pilot, payload
S	Site, size, shape, slope, surface, sun, surrounds, stock
W	Wind, wires, wires, wires, way in, way out
A	Approval
T	Turning and termination

Combinations

Below are two examples that are a combination of an abbreviation, acronym and a mnemonic.

KISS (Keep It Simple Stupid)

- Abbreviation (is a shortened word or phrase)
- Acronym (is formed from the initials)
- Mnemonic (is said as a word)

ASAP (As Soon As Possible)

- Abbreviation
- Acronym (Said as "A.S.A.P.")
- Mnemonic (Said as "A SAP")

Callsigns and Identifiers

All aircraft and vehicles used in aviation have a unique callsign to identify them on the radio. Just like cars on the road must have license plates so the police and other authorities can identify them.

A callsign might be a word that is registered with Air Traffic Control. For example, British Airways uses the callsign "Speedbird".

Alternatively, and more frequently for small aircraft, a callsign is based on the aircraft registration number.

Aircraft Registration Callsigns

Countries have different standards for callsigns. Generally, every country has a set of letters assigned by ICAO, which are placed ahead of the registration number. For example:

VH	Australia
ZK	New Zealand
N	United States
B	China / Hong Kong
PK	Indonesia
HZ	Saudi Arabia
A6	United Arab Emirates
9V	Singapore
A7	Qatar
A9C	Bahrain

The initial country prefix may be followed by a combination of numbers and/or letters.

In Australia, aircraft have 3 letters registrations. For example:

- VH-PIH
- VH-TRW
- VH-RNX
- VH-RZQ

During radio calls, an aircraft callsign can be made up from:

- Aircraft Registration including the country pre-fix, for example:
  - VH-PIH (called as Papa India Hotel)
  - N3456L (called as November three fower fife six Lima [full version] or fife six Lima [short version])
- The aircraft Type / Make / Model for example:
  - Helicopter PIH
  - R22 RZQ
  - Cessna 172 OLR
- Registered Callsigns and flight numbers (commonly used for airlines like Qantas) for example:
  - Qantas 122 "heavy" (for QF122) called as Qantas One Twenty-Two Heavy or Qantas One Twenty-Two Hotel
  - Saudi 345 (for SV345) called as Saudi Three Forty-Five

Some aircraft may use the term "heavy" (or "hotel") after their callsign. This relates to the aircraft's total weight and identifies the aircraft as having "wake turbulence" that needs to be considered by pilots and air traffic control when planning the separation of aircraft (the time between arrivals and departures).

Vehicle Callsigns

Vehicles operating on the airport apron may also have callsigns. The numbers are pronounced in full:

- Car 15 is called Car Fifteen
- Rescue 12 is called Rescue Twelve
- Fire Engine 2 is called Fire Two

Runways and Taxiways

Runways are assigned numbers, for example:

- Runway 36   (Runway Three Six)
- Runway 18   (Runway One Eight)

There may be parallel runways, in which case they are called Left, Centre and Right, for example:

- Runway 17L   (Runway One Seven Left)
- Runway 17R   (Runway One Seven Right)

Taxiways are assigned letters, for example:

- Taxiway A   (Taxiway Alpha)
- Taxiway B   (Taxiway Bravo)

A Taxiway may have numbers; for example, if Taxiway Bravo has 2 exits, they may be numbered B1 and B2:

- Taxiway B1   (Taxiway Bravo One)
- Taxiway B2   (Taxiway Bravo Two)

Standard shorthand

The following shorthand is a suggested format that will allow the crew to quickly write down information in a short version on the kneeboard.

Word or phrase	Abbreviation
Above	ABV
Below	BLW
Altitude 5000 (At 5000)	A050
Above 5000	A050 (underlined)
Below 5000	A050 (overlined)
Cruise	→
Before	>
After	<
Climb to 5000	↑A050
Descend to 5000	↓A050
Enter control area	(arrow into triangle)
Out of (leave) control area	(arrow out of triangle)
While in a control area	△
Contact	CTC
Report	R
Reporting point	REP
Remain well to the left-hand side	LS
Remain well to the right-hand side	RS
Left turn after take-off	↰

Word or phrase	Abbreviation
Right turn after take-off	↱
Left hand / right hand	LH / RH
Cross	X
Advise	ADV
Squawk	SQ
Heading	HDG
Magnetic	MAG
Maintain	MNT
Direct	DCT
Take off (direction)	(N)
Go via	VIA
Tower	TWR
Runway (number EG 18)	RWY18
Cleared to Land	L
Final	F
Flight planned route	FPR
From	FM
Until	U
Until further advised	UFA

Mike Becker, Becker Helicopters

Understanding Airspace

Aim

This chapter aims to review:

- The different categories of airspace; and
- What equipment and radio calls are required in each of the different airspace categories

Introduction to Airspace

Knowing how to use the radio is one thing; knowing when to use it and who you should be talking to is another.

When flying, we are either in an environment:

- that is controlled by an Air Traffic Controller, or
- where there is no control and we take responsibility for all of our actions and radio calls.

Airspace is primarily divided into those areas where there are:

- high-capacity jets with hundreds of people on board requiring separation and increased levels of safety; and
- smaller aircraft that only have a few people on board and are essentially uncontrolled and do not require such a high level of safety.

(Landesman, 2010 [Modified])

The level of guidance, support and control depends on where the most risk is.

Australian Flight Information Region

Every country in the world is responsible for a section or sections of airspace. These sections of airspace usually encompass the country but may also include territories or outer islands.

Australia is responsible for airspace surrounding Australia, parts of the Antarctic and some remote islands, including Lord Howe and Norfolk Islands. This entire area is referred to as the **Australian Flight Information Region (FIR)**.

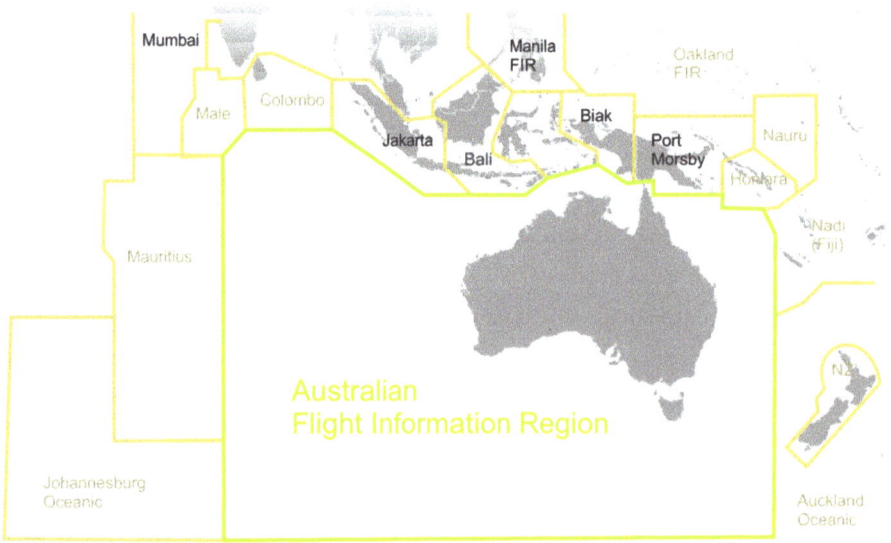

Any Airspace that is **within 12NM** of the Australian mainland is known as **Domestic Airspace**.

Any Airspace **outside of the 12NM** distance from any part of the Australian mainland (including islands) is known as **Oceanic or International Airspace**, and the flight must be on an International flight plan.

Australian Communication Centres

In Australia, there are two (2) communication centres where controllers are located to monitor and communicate via radio and satellite with aircraft.

1. One is located in Brisbane and is responsible for the northern half of Australia and is called **Brisbane Centre**.
2. The second communication centre is located in Melbourne and is responsible for the southern half of Australia and all the airspace in the Southern Ocean to Antarctica and is called **Melbourne Centre**.

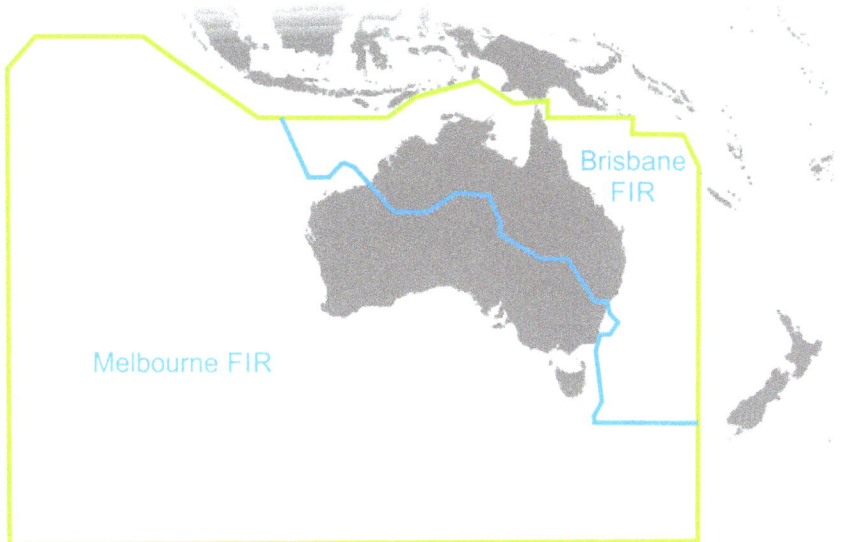

The Brisbane and Melbourne FIRs are then divided into smaller areas called Flight Information Areas (FIAs) based on the reception of VHF and HF radio and the associated repeater stations and antennas that have been installed.

These boundaries are found on the aviation charts (PCA, ERC, VNC and VTC) so that pilots can plan and then tune in to the correct frequency while flying.

All communication eventually ends up in one of these two centres.

Classes of Airspace

Each country may define its classes of airspace and associated rules based on standards defined by ICAO. In Australia, the Classes A, C, D, E and G of airspace are used, as follows:

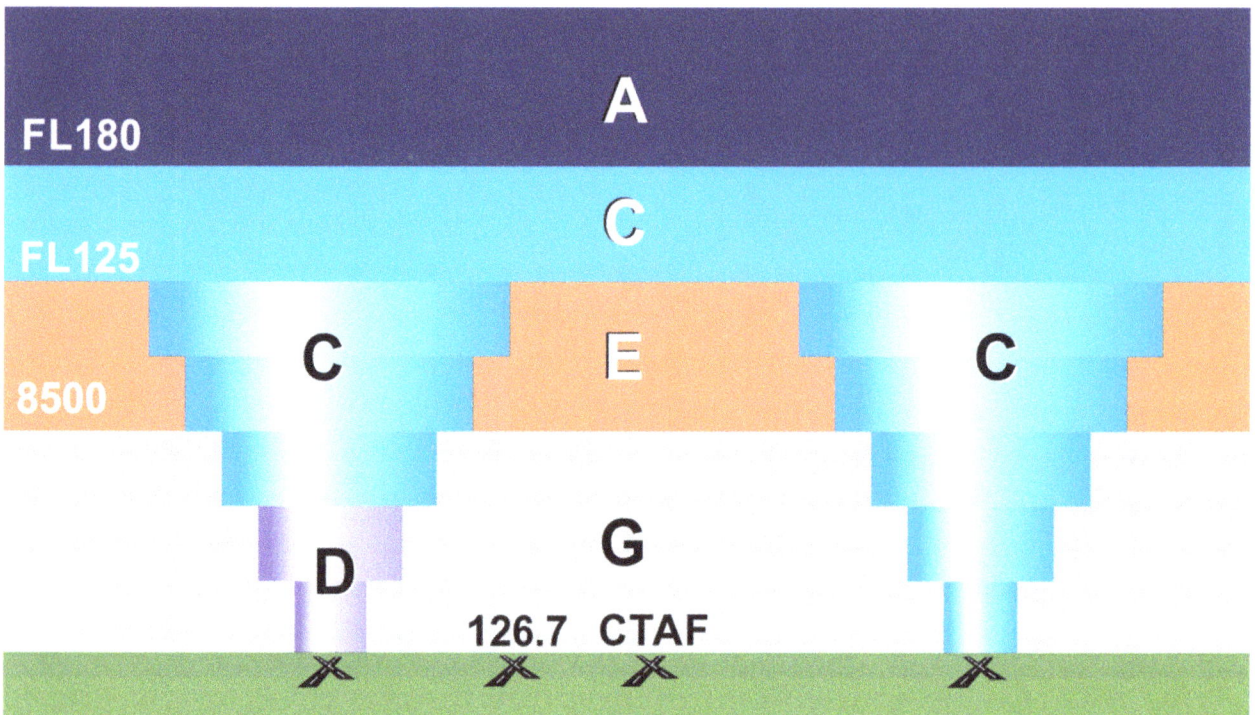

Class	Type	Level	Category	Radio required	Transponder required	Airways Clearance
A	Controlled	Above FL180	IFR only	Yes	Yes	Yes
C	Controlled	FL125 – FL180	IFR | VFR	Yes	Yes	Yes
D	Controlled	Surface to 4500 ft	IFR | VFR	Yes	Yes	Yes
E*	Controlled (IFR) | Uncontrolled (VFR)	8500 ft – FL125	IFR | VFR	Yes	Yes	Yes (IFR) | No (VFR)
G	Uncontrolled	Below 8500 ft	IFR | VFR	No	No	No

* Class E airspace may be at various levels depending on where it is in Australia. Class E commonly starts at 8500 feet. Aircrews consult the various maps and the AIP to get the exact levels in the areas they are flying.

In addition to the standard classes of airspace, there are also special use airspace types which include:

- Military airspace
- Air Defence Identification Zone (ADIZ)
- Prohibited, Restricted and Danger area (PRD).

Military Airspace

Military-controlled airspace still comes under the banner of Class A, C, D, E or G. The main point of difference is that the military is responsible for managing aircraft within their airspace instead of Air Services, so they prioritise military aircraft and not civil aircraft.

If entering or transiting military airspace, the same procedures apply as for the normal airspace. The key difference is that the military can deny your request and you will then have to go around or find another way to get to your destination. In most cases, the military controllers are very accommodating, but all crew should read the NOTAMs before a flight to determine the hours of service and any special procedures.

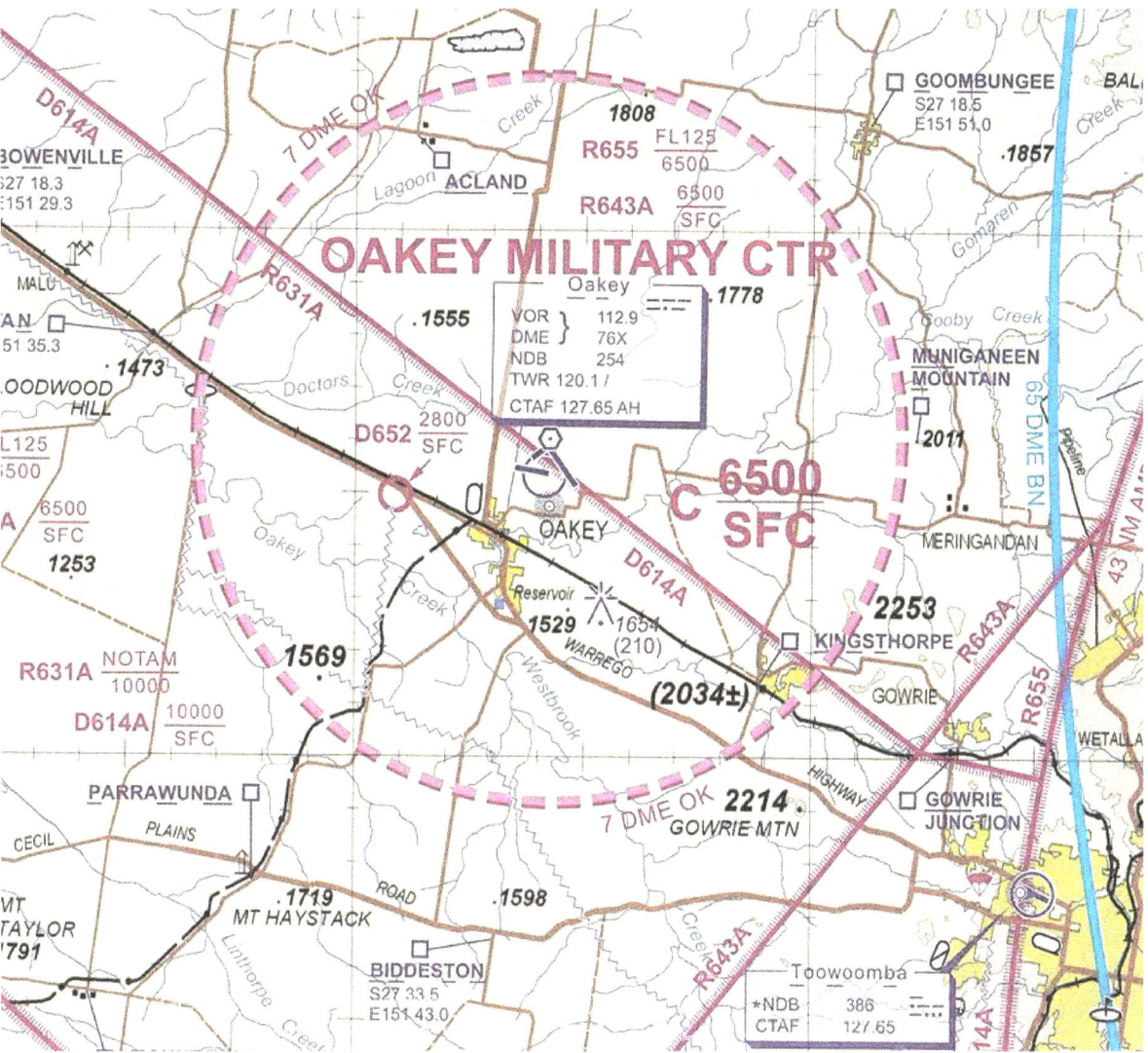

Air Defence Identification Zone (ADIZ)

An Air Defence Identification Zone (ADIZ) is special-purpose airspace that the military can create anywhere at any time in the event of a major requirement. They are rare but may be created during an emergency or special event.

For full ADIZ procedures, see the AIP or VFG.

Example
Consider a country hosting the G20 summit of all government leaders. The military may set up a special ADIZ around the meeting area. This invokes special procedures, radio calls and planning for a short period while the ADIZ is active.

The Military always controls an ADIZ.

Example
Below is an example of an ADIZ established in Perth during a meeting of government leaders in 2011. 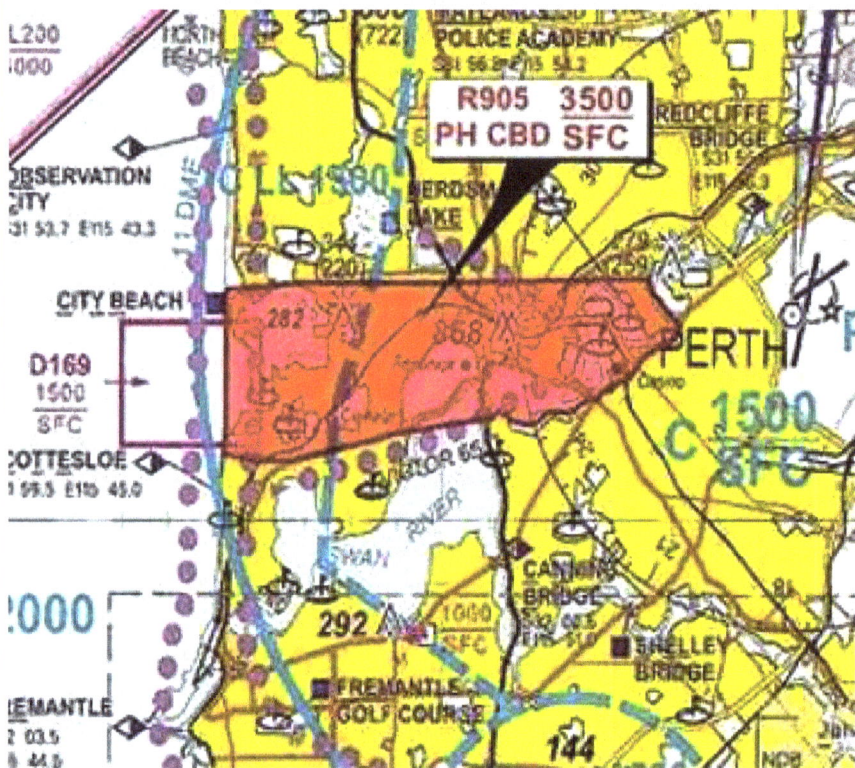 The above ADIZ consisted of three (3) Temporary Restricted Areas (TRA) that were activated by NOTAM and patrolled by both defence and police aircraft: - R905 covered the Perth CBD area - R906 covered inner Perth out to 11 DME - R907 went out to 36 DME from Perth. Any operations within these areas during the time of activation were with the permission of the military.

For further information on how to operate within an ADIZ, consult the ERSA emergency pages.

Prohibited, Restricted and Danger (PRD) Areas

Prohibited, **Restricted** and **Danger** (PRD) Areas are designated airspace where specific conditions, rules or procedures apply. Information can be found in the PRD section of the ERSA.

Restricted Areas

Prohibited and Restricted areas are combined into a tiered restricted format as follows:

- Restricted Area 1 (RA1)
- Restricted Area 2 (RA2)
- Restricted Area 3 (RA3).

The term Prohibited Area is no longer used.

RA1

RA1 is a Restricted Area where the entry or transit of aircraft may be restricted.

This means there are times when they are active and permission is required to enter them. When they are not active, they can be treated like Class G airspace.

In RA1, pilots may flight plan through the Restricted Area and expect a clearance from ATC under normal circumstances.

RA2

RA2 is a Restricted Area where the entry or transit of aircraft may be restricted, similar to RA1.

This means there are times when they are active and permission is required to enter them. When they are not active, they can be treated like Class G airspace.

In RA2, pilots must not plan a flight through the restricted area when active unless on a route specified in ERSA GEN FPR or under agreement with the Department of Defence.

Even if given permission prior, a clearance from ATC is not assured on arrival, and alternative tracking may be offered through the restricted area.

RA3

RA3 is a Restricted Area where the entry of aircraft is **prohibited**.

In RA3, pilots must not plan a flight through the restricted area and ATC clearances are not available.

PRD Areas on Charts

On aviation charts, each Restricted Area has a reference number and has a combined border of solid red and broken red. Information about the restricted area is found in the ERSA. The key thing to remember is that aircraft can fly in a restricted area when active, but only with permission and with restrictions. If they are not active, then they can be treated like Class G airspace.

Example of a PRD areas on a chart

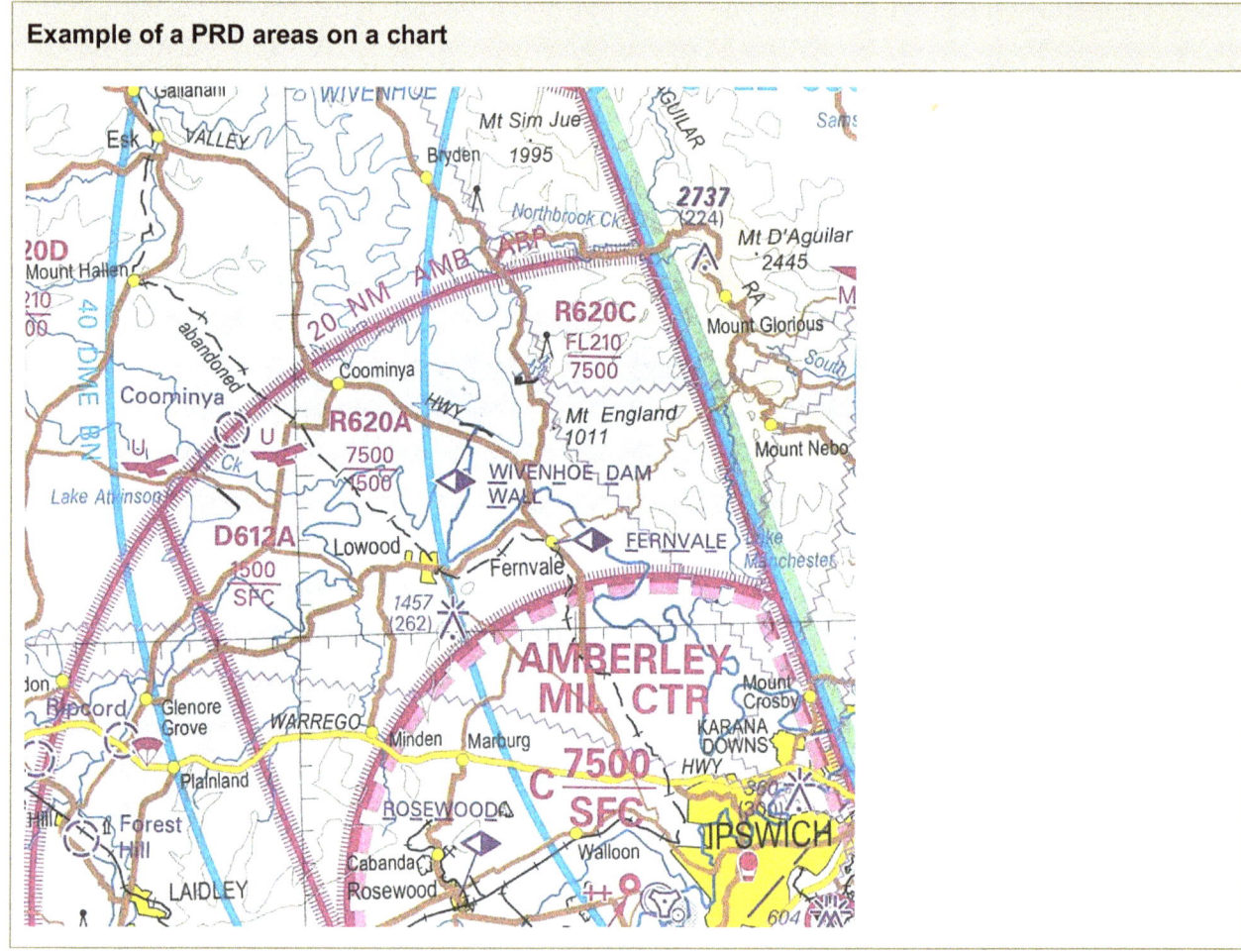

Danger

A Danger Area warns pilots that there is something extra to look out for and be aware of. There are no special radio procedures and there are no restrictions for flying in or through these areas. On aviation charts, the Danger Area will have a reference number and is bounded by a red line. Information about each Danger Area is available in the ERSA.

> **Example**
>
> An area that is commonly used by other aircraft for training may be marked as a Danger Area as all aircraft transiting through the area need to be extra vigilant and look out for training aircraft. The example below shows three danger areas: D629A, D629B and D629C.
>
>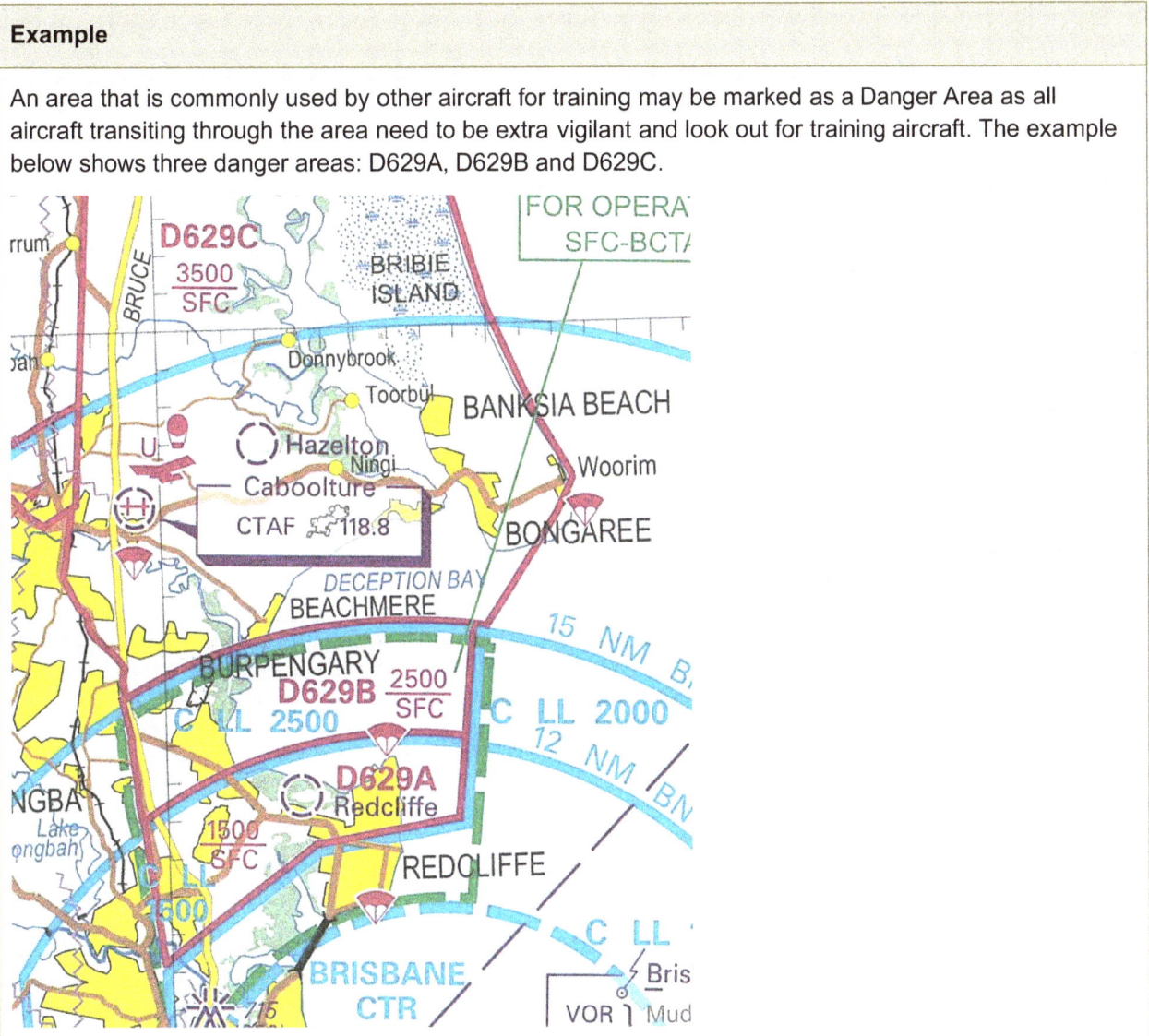

Difference between CTA and CTR

There is a difference in definition and procedure depending on what type of controlled airspace the aircraft is required to enter.

1. A **Controlled Area (CTA)** always requires an airways clearance and will have a higher level of control. It may or may not have radar surveillance and can be designated as either Class A, Class C, Class D or Class E (for IFR) airspace.
2. A **Control Zone (CTR)** can have different requirements depending on whether it is designated Class C or Class D airspace as follows:
   (a) **Class C CTR** always requires an airways clearance and is under radar surveillance.
   (b) **Class D CTR** still requires an airways clearance, but it may be implied and there is no radar surveillance. Although there is a lower level of control, there is a higher-level requirement to abide by procedures and rely on radio communication for separation.

Control Area (CTA)

A Control Area (CTA) is defined as controlled airspace that starts at a specified height above the earth's surface upwards to a specified upper limit. Any vertical upper and lower limits and lateral dimensions of the CTA area are marked on the VTC, VNC and ERC charts.

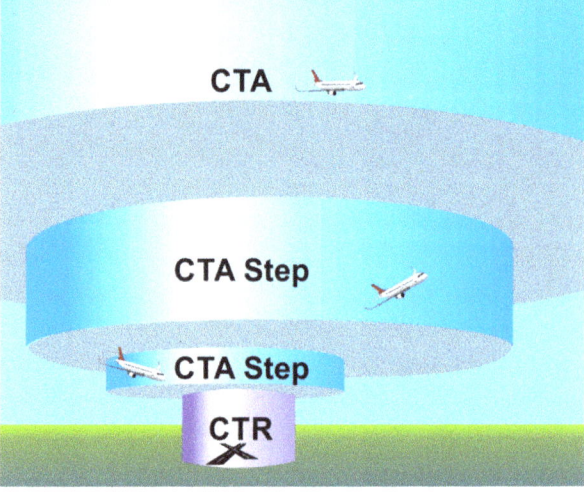

All operations within a Control Area must be done so in accordance with published procedures and all aircraft require an Airways Clearance, except for VFR aircraft in Class E airspace.

Control Zones (CTR)

A Control Zone (CTR) is defined as controlled airspace that starts at the ground (Surface or SFC) and extends upwards to a specified limit above the earth's surface. Any vertical upper and lower limits, as well as any lateral dimensions of the CTR, are marked on the VTC, VNC and ERC charts.

Control Zones (CTRs) surround aerodromes that are controlled by the Tower controller in:

- Class C airspace;
- Class D airspace; and
- Military control zones.

Example of a CTR that has increasing CTA steps around it and above it.

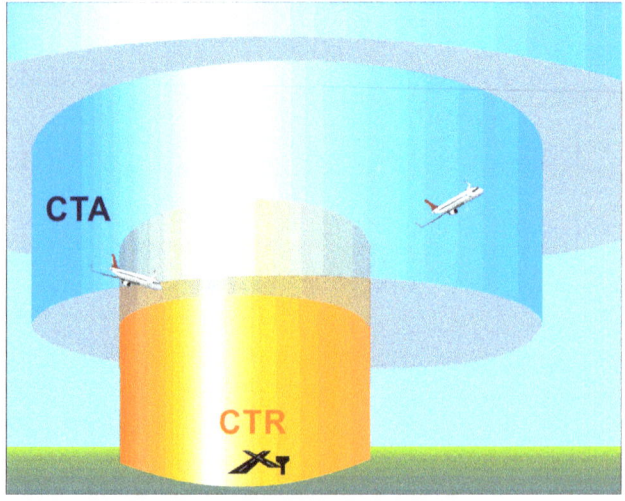

Aviation Communication and Flight Radio *for Helicopter Pilots*

Example of a CTR with a CTA step the same size above it along with increasing CTA steps above it.

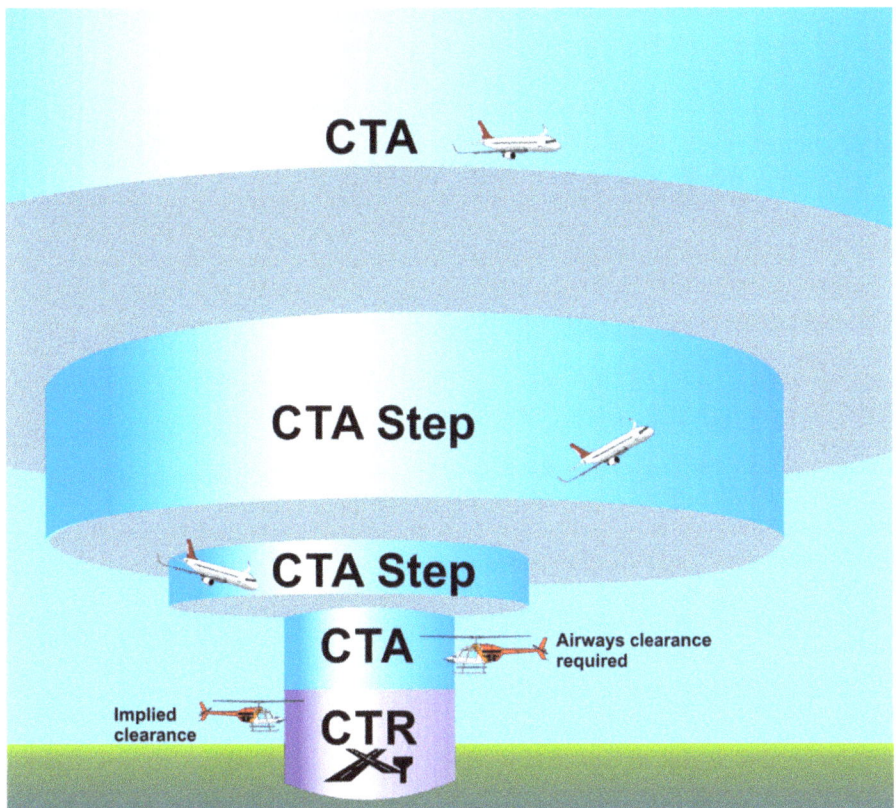

All operations within a Control Zone must be done so in accordance with published procedures and all aircraft require an Airways Clearance. However, aerodromes in Class D airspace have an additional option to operate on an *implied clearance,* if only operating in the Control Zone and not entering an associated Control Area.

Implied Clearance

In some control zones within Class D Airspace, the airspace is divided into two (2) parts.

- one part is considered a **Control Zone (CTR),** and then
- when climbing past a specified height, it becomes a **Control Area (CTA)**.

If the pilot wants to enter or depart the Control Zone and remain below the Control Area, they simply have to tell the Tower Controller what they want to do. If the Tower Controller agrees, they read back the aircraft's callsign and no further communication is required. This is an implied airways clearance, where the full airways clearance is not spoken, but it is agreed to have been given by acknowledgement. The acknowledgement is deemed to have been given if the Tower controller reads back the aircraft's callsign after the aircraft has made a call with intentions. If the controller does not agree with what the pilot has said, they may come back with amendments or limits.

The logic behind this is to save radio chatter in busy Class D aerodromes.

If the pilot intends on entering the Control Area above the Control Zone, then a full spoken airways clearance and readback is required.

> **Example**
>
> Consider the airspace immediately above the Sunshine Coast Airport. Looking at the VTC image below, there are three (3) notations in BLUE regarding airspace.
>
> - D SFC to 1500
> - D LL 1500, and
> - C LL 4500
>
>
>
> Where:
>
> - D SFC to 1500 means
>   Class D airspace CTR (Control Zone) starts at the surface and stops at 1500 feet AMSL.
>   Class D Upper Limit of the CTR is 1500 feet AMSL
> - D LL 1500 means
>   Class D Lower Limit of the CTA (Control Area) starts at 1500 feet AMSL and ends at 4500 feet AMSL
> - C LL 4500 means
>   Class C Lower Limit of the CTA starts at 4500 feet AMSL and continues up by the remaining steps.
>
> In plain language, the Class D Control Zone (CTR) extends upwards from the surface (SFC) to 1500 feet, this airspace is controlled by the Sunshine Coast Tower controller.
>
> Then the Class D Control Area (CTA) starts at 1500 feet and extends upwards to 4500 feet, this airspace is still controlled by the Sunshine Coast Tower controller.
>
> After that the Control Area (CTA) changes to Class C airspace and continues upwards in accordance with the remaining CTA steps, this airspace is controlled by the Brisbane Centre controller.

Interpreting this can be confusing and takes some practice.

Radar at Airports

Radar environment

When flying near a major airport that has Primary and Secondary Radar, the radio communication within the Class C environment is less. This is because the Air Traffic Controller can see you on the radar screens and does not require a full radio call with all the information when they already know most of it. This means a radar-controlled aerodrome can facilitate many more aircraft with significantly less radio communication.

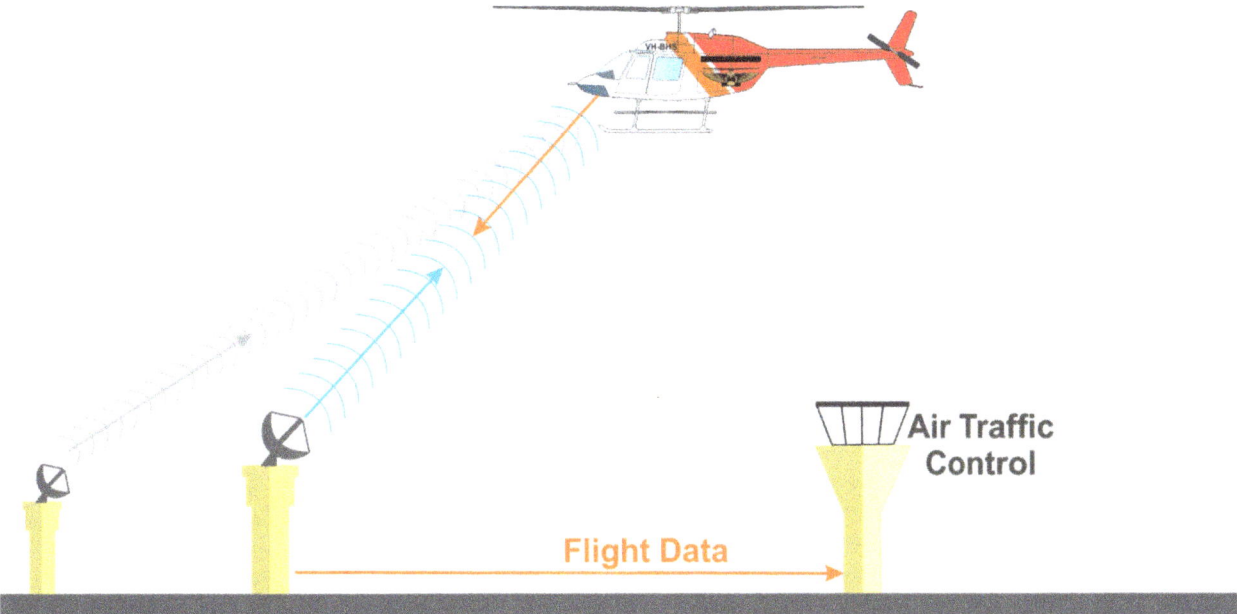

Primary radar:
No flight data.
Can only show approximate position.

Secondary radar:
Tracks plane and its identify via transponder

Primary radar: Consists of a ground-based radar sending out a signal and picking up an object in the air, whether it has a transponder installed or not. The range for a primary radar is typically no more than 50NM from the radar station.

Secondary radar: Secondary radar relies on a signal sent from the ground-based radar interrogated by a transponder unit in the aircraft. The transponder unit sends a pulsed signal back to the radar with embedded information, such as pressure altitude, transponder code and an indication of position. This is known as secondary surveillance radar (SSR) and has a much greater range (over 250 nm for a land-based unit and unlimited if it is via satellite).

Example
Brisbane International Airport is a Class C Radar controlled airport.

Non-Radar Environment

When flying near an aerodrome with no radar facilities, the radio communication will increase as the Air Traffic Controller requires the pilot to communicate all the relevant information by radio to get a clear picture of where all the aircraft are under their control and how to keep them separated. The pilot is also required to readback any height, heading, transponder code or clearance that ATC gives, so in effect, the radio communication is now doubled.

The use of this airspace is referred to as a *"Procedural Aerodrome"* and the radio traffic can become very congested very quickly. A Procedural Aerodrome can only handle a limited number of aircraft simultaneously, due to the amount of communication work required.

Aerodrome with no radar facilities relies on radio communications.

Example
Sunshine Coast Airport is a Class D Procedural airport.

Maps and Charts

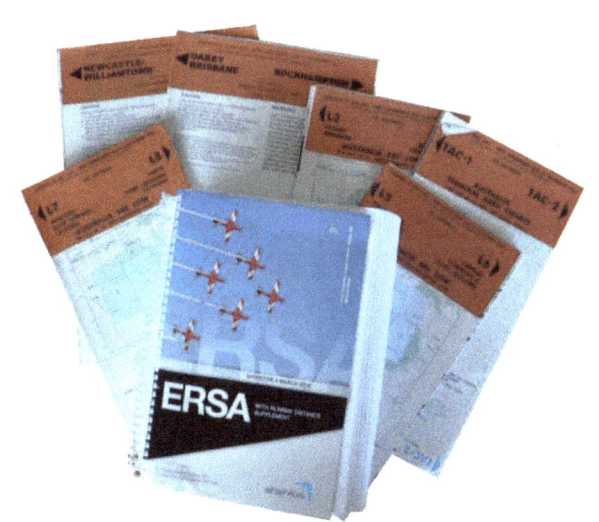

Major airports have maps and charts that depict the airspace for use by the crew when flying. The most common charts for VFR operations are the VTC (Visual Terminal Chart) and the VNC (Visual Navigation Chart).

The most common charts for IFR are the TAC (Terminal Area Chart) and the ERC (Enroute Chart).

Minor non-towered airports often have minimal information on a map; most of the information required will be found in the ERSA.

These charts are amended and then updated every six (6) months; any changes to the airspace boundaries will be shown on these charts. It is very important that the crew have the most up to date documents, maps and charts, so the aircraft is not accidentally flown into controlled airspace without making the appropriate radio calls at the right times.

In the planning stages of a flight, it is important that these charts are reviewed when deciding, *before* the flight, where to make radios calls and to whom.

Common abbreviations used on the maps

The table below defines the meaning of common abbreviations used on the maps.

Abbreviation	Meaning
LL	Lower Limit of the airspace
SFC	Surface (from ground level or 0 feet)
FL	Flight Level When FL is used, then the height is divided by 100. **Example**: - FL180 = 18,000 feet - FL125 = 12,500 feet This is commonly used for levels over 10,000 feet.
CTR	Controlled Zone; begins at the surface. The airspace boundary on charts for a Controlled Zone has a **dashed** line.
CTA	Controlled Area; begins above the surface. The airspace boundary on charts for a Controlled Area has a **solid** line.

Understanding the Map Markings

Let's take a closer look at the map to understand how you identify different classes of airspace.

Examples
 **A LL FL180** A = Class A Airspace LL FL180 = Lower Limit is 18,000 feet **C LL 8500** C = Class C Airspace LL 8500 = Lower Limit is 8,500 feet
 **C LL 7500** C = Class C Airspace LL 7500 = Lower Limit is 7,500 feet
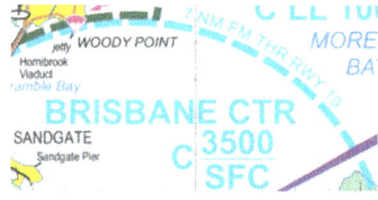 **C 3500 / SFC** C = Class C Airspace SFC = Lower Limit is the ground or 0 feet. 3500 = Upper Limit is 3,500 feet. Airspace that has a surface (SFC) lower limit is a Controlled Zone (CTR). Notice the border around the CTR airspace boundary has **dashes**.

Examples

C LL 3500

C = Class C Airspace

LL 3500 = Lower Limit is 3,500 feet.

This falls within the CTR airspace boundary (shown with **dashes**). Therefore, the airspace from 3,500 feet and above the CTR (Controlled Zone) is a Class C CTA (Controlled Area).

C LL 2000

Class C has a Lower Limit of 2000 feet.

Notice that the border has a **solid** line indicating a CTA (Controlled Area).

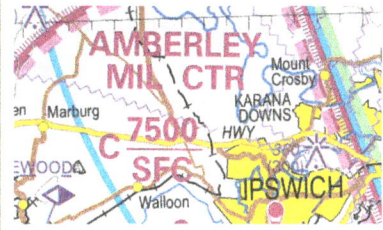

MIL CTR
C 7500/SFC

MIL CTR = Military Control Zone

C = Class C Airspace

SFC = Lower Limit is the surface

7500 = Upper Limit is 7,500 feet

Notice that the boundary is a red **dashed** line, indicating a Military Control Zone.

Examples

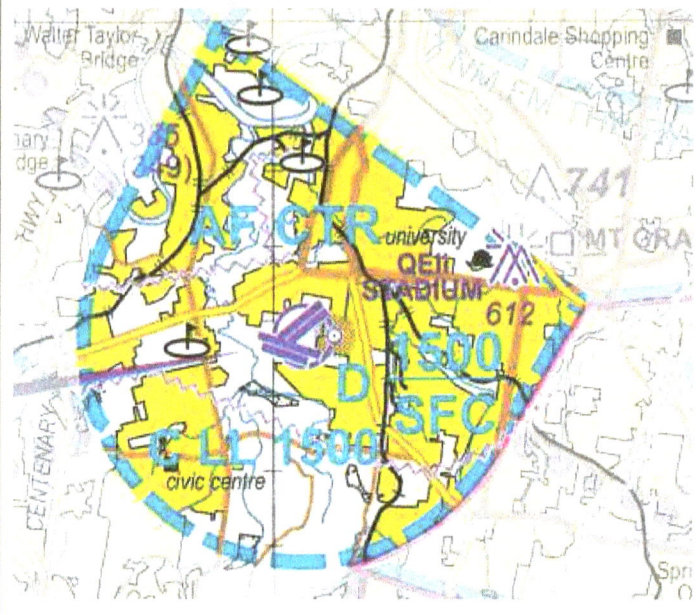

D $\frac{1500}{SFC}$

D = Class D Airspace

SFC = Lower Limit is the surface

1500 = Upper Limit is 1,500 feet

This is a CTR because it starts at the SFC, it has a dashed border, and it is marked as AF (Archerfield) CTR on the map.

C LL 1500

C = Class C Airspace

LL 1500 = Lower Limit is 1,500 feet.

This indicates that the airspace above the Class D CTR is a Class C CTA.

Aviation Communication and Flight Radio *for Helicopter Pilots*

Review of the Sunshine Coast VTC

Below is an extract from the Sunshine Coast VTC with some of the markings explained.

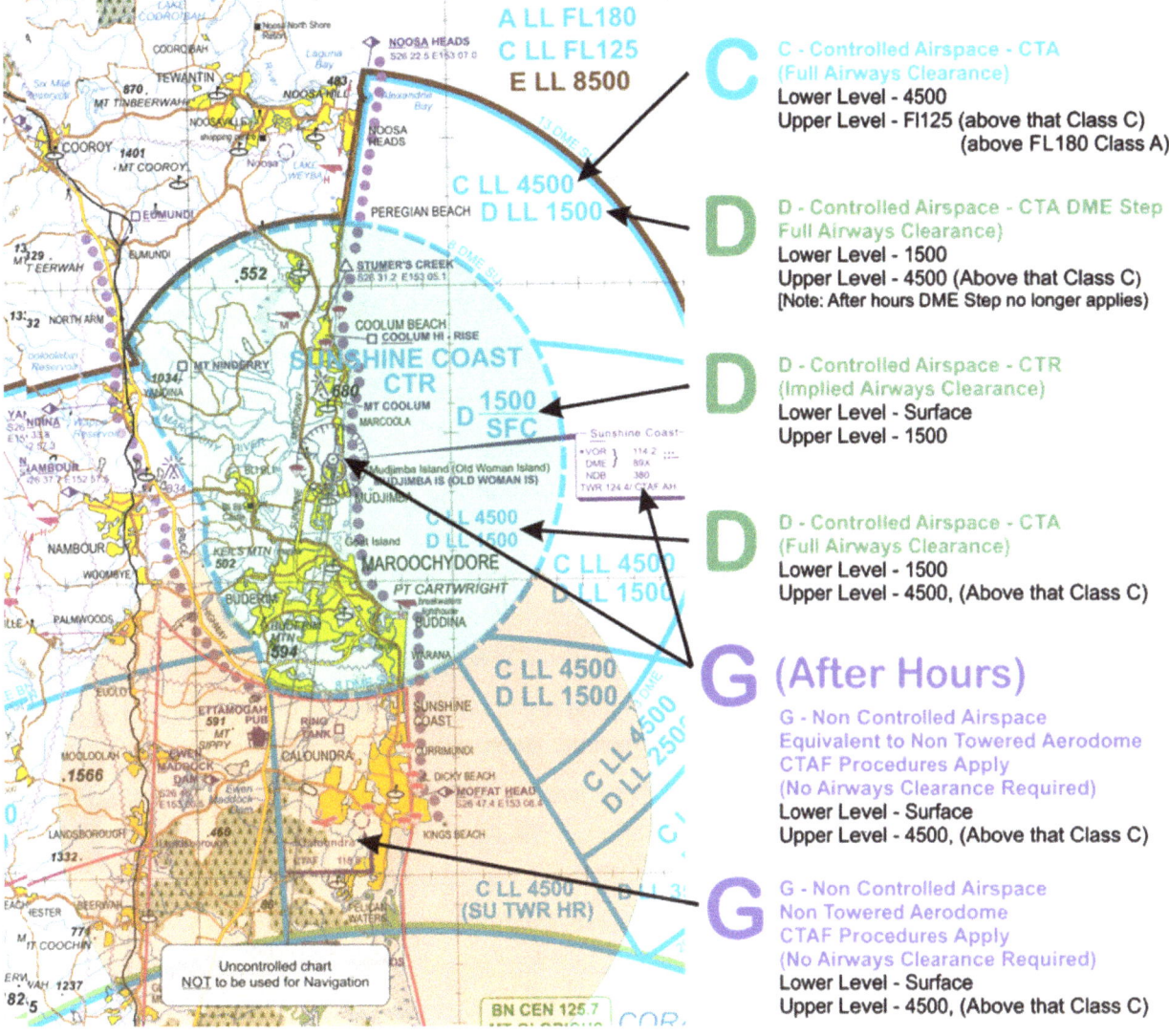

Mike Becker, Becker Helicopters

Review of the Brisbane VNC

Below is an extract from the Brisbane VNC with some abbreviations explained.

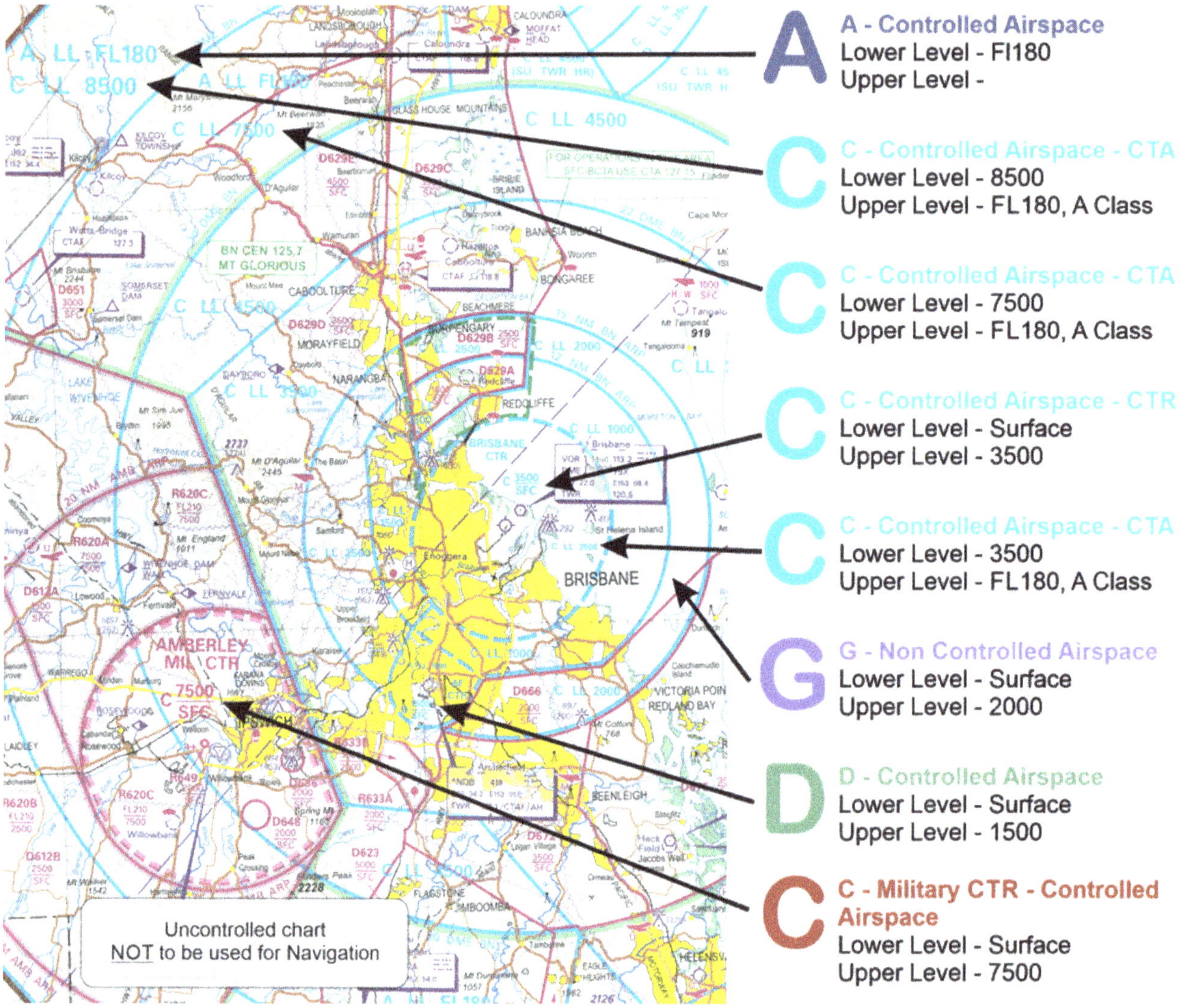

A - Controlled Airspace
Lower Level - Fl180
Upper Level -

C - Controlled Airspace - CTA
Lower Level - 8500
Upper Level - FL180, A Class

C - Controlled Airspace - CTA
Lower Level - 7500
Upper Level - FL180, A Class

C - Controlled Airspace - CTR
Lower Level - Surface
Upper Level - 3500

C - Controlled Airspace - CTA
Lower Level - 3500
Upper Level - FL180, A Class

G - Non Controlled Airspace
Lower Level - Surface
Upper Level - 2000

D - Controlled Airspace
Lower Level - Surface
Upper Level - 1500

C - Military CTR - Controlled Airspace
Lower Level - Surface
Upper Level - 7500

The diagram below illustrates the different areas of the Brisbane VNC and Sunshine Coast VTC from the side view. This demonstrates the stepping up of the Class C airspace and the associated Class C and Class D CTRs for the aerodromes indicated in the previous maps.

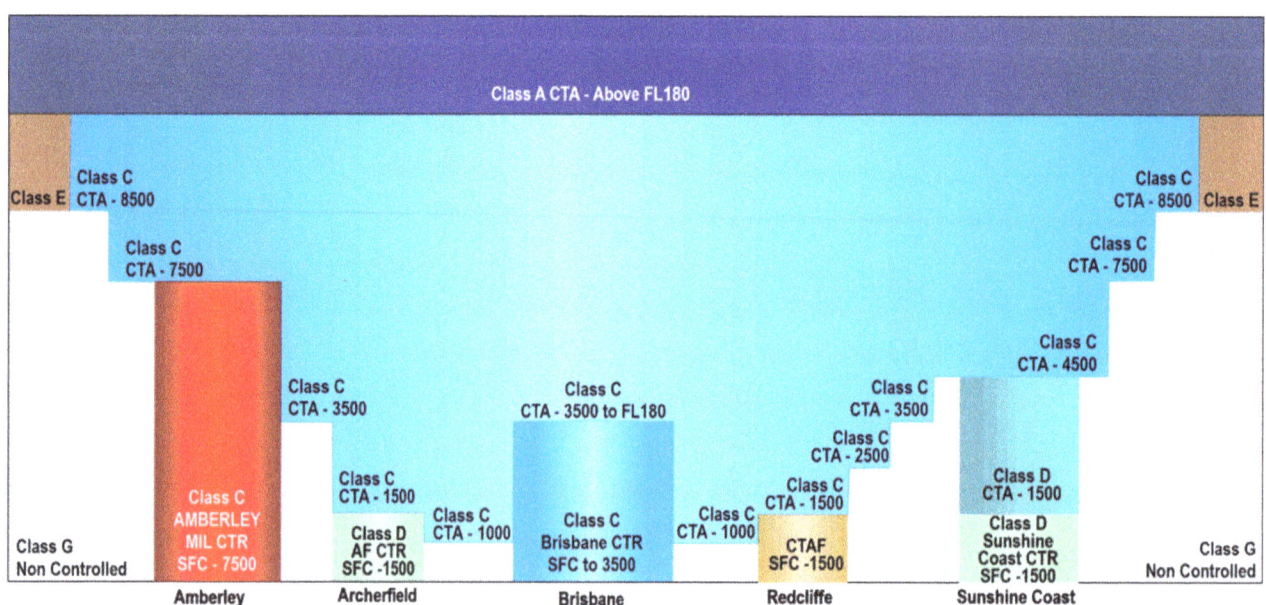

Page 58

Radio Procedures Overview

Aim

This chapter aims to introduce the trainee to:

- Radio technique and etiquette
- When to call and who to call.

Related documents

- Aviation English course notes and presentations
- Aviation Law course notes
- ERSA, maps and charts
- AIP GEN 3.4

Introduction

The previous chapters have now set you up to have a solid foundation and understanding of the radio.

In this chapter, we are going to put it all together and discuss how to find the right frequency, how to make the right radio call at the right time.

Using the principles in this chapter will help you sound like a professional on the radio and make and receive radio calls with confidence.

This chapter describes:

- Who to Call
- When to Call
- How to Call.

Following is a quick overview of radio procedures, which will be covered in more detail in later chapters.

Types of Radio Calls

There are three main types of radio calls used in aviation:

- **Calls** – to specific stations or aircraft, for example, when requesting information
- **Reports** – to a specific air traffic control service
- **Broadcasts** – to advise others of your location and intentions.

Procedure

When making a radio call, you need to:

- Ensure you have the right frequency selected
- Listen out on the frequency to be used and avoid interfering with other transmissions
- Plan what you are going to say
- Press the "press to talk" (PTT) button
- Speak into the microphone
- When finished speaking, release the PTT button

Pronunciation and Voice Control

It is important to make sure the person you are talking to can understand you, so make sure that you:

- pronounce each word clearly
- have a slight pause before and after transmitting numbers to help the accuracy of reception
- keep your volume moderate and constant
- speak slightly slowly
- use the standard words and phrases
- use the phonetic alphabet.

Initiating a Call

Think of initiating a call like making a phone call. When you call someone on the phone, you first make sure you are talking to the right person. There is nothing worse than talking to the wrong person on the phone.

Once you are sure you are talking to the right person, you need to let them know who you are and the reason you are calling.

Initiating a call

Hi, is that Jane?
This is John.
Do you want to
go to the cinema
tonight?

Responding to a call

Hi John.
Yes, this is Jane.
I would love to
go to the cinema
tonight.

The standard sequence for making a radio call is as follows:

- **Who you are calling**
- **Who you are**
  (Say "HELICOPTER" before the callsign then the type of helicopter. If you are talking to the tower/ground, add the Persons On Board (POB) number and the ATIS letter received.)
- **Where you are**
  (if relevant –altitude, position, heading)
  and
- **What you want to do**
  or
- **What you want to know**.

Example
A pilot would initiate a call as follows: *"Sunshine Coast Ground* *Helicopter Whiskey Charlie Juliet, Bell 206, 2 POB, received Alpha* *At Becker South* *Request taxi to Pad Bravo"*

Aviation Communication and Flight Radio *for Helicopter Pilots*

Responding to a Call

When responding to a radio call, you want to tell the person calling that you have heard them, using their callsign, and that they are talking to the right person before you carry on with your message.

The standard sequence for responding to a radio call is as follows:

- **Who you are talking to** (who made the initiating call)
- **Who you are**
- **The message**

Example
The call from Ground/Tower would be: *"Whisky Charlie Juliet*   *Sunshine Coast Ground*   *Cleared to taxi via Golf to Pad Bravo"*

Established Communication

Once communication is established, you may simplify a radio call. For example, when sending a message, you may simply state:

- The aircraft/callsign involved
- The message

Example
The pilot might say something like this: *"Whiskey Charlie Juliet*   *"Cleared to taxi via Golf to Pad Bravo"*   Note: Only the callsign is repeated; there is no need to repeat Tower/Ground

Corrections

To make a correction during a radio call, use the word "correction".

Example
The pilot might say something like this: *"Whiskcy Charlie Juliet*   *Time two niner*   *Correction three niner"*

Clearances and Readbacks

To make sure that you have heard the message correctly, we make a readback call. You need to provide a full readback call when we have been given:

- an airways clearance, or
- any amendments to instructions previously given.

For example, readbacks are required in the following situations:

- All clearances and instructions to hold short of, cross, enter, land on, takeoff from, line-up on and taxi or backtrack on any runway
- Assigned runway, altimeter settings, transponder codes, and frequency details
- Level instructions, direction of turn, heading and speed instructions
- En route holding instructions
- Any holding point specified in a taxi clearance
- Any approach clearance.

Example 1

A radio call from Tower to Pilot:

Tower: "Whiskey Charlie Juliet Cleared for Training Area Bravo, not above 500"

Pilot: "Cleared for Training Area Bravo, not above 500, Whiskey Charlie Juliet"

Example 2

A radio call from Tower to Pilot:

Tower: "Tango Romeo Whiskey, Descend to and maintain two thousand"

Pilot: "Descend to and maintain two thousand, Tango Romeo Whiskey"

Who to call

Air Traffic Control (ATC) has differing service levels depending on the frequency of aircraft and the type of operation.

Since Regular Public Transport (RPT) aircraft carry hundreds of fare-paying passengers at a time, they are given the highest level of ATC service and support to provide the highest levels of safety.

(Landesman, 2010)

This service and support are based around:

- major airports where these RPT aircraft land and take-off, and
- at the higher altitudes where they fly.

The closer you get to a major airport, the lower the controlled airspace is, as these larger aircraft are taking off and landing, so they need the airspace to make the climb and descent. The further away from a major airport and the lower you fly, the lower the level of ATC service until there is none and you are on your own.

The busier the airport, the more the tasks are divided by ATC so that the radio is not congested. Below is a list of tasks that are required from a busy airport to outside controlled airspace:

- Recorded messages, including:
    - Automatic Terminal Information Service (ATIS)
    - Aerodrome Weather Information: AWIS or AWIB
    - Automatical Enroute Information Service (AERIS)
- Airways Clearance Delivery (ACD)
- Surface Movement Control (Ground)
- Tower
- Departures
- Approach
- Flight Information Area (FIA)
- Flight Information Service (FIS)
- Unicom
- Non-towered aerodromes and OCTA

At airports that are not busy, then two or more of these tasks may be combined into one unit and managed by one (1) controller instead of two (2) or three (3).

> **Example**
>
> When calling Ground at the Sunshine Coast, a taxi clearance and possibly an airways clearance is given. This is because Ground is doing the job of both the Ground controller and the ACD controller.
>
> At Brisbane, the Ground clearance and the Airways Clearance will be on two (2) separate frequencies requiring pilots to talk to two (2) different controllers who are located in different rooms.

Recorded messages

There are several automatic information services, including:

- Automatic Terminal Information Service (ATIS)
- Aerodrome Weather Information: AWIS or AWIB
- Automatical Enroute Information Service (AERIS)

Automatic Terminal Information Service (ATIS)

The Automatic Terminal Information Service (ATIS) frequency can be found in ERSA and is commonly referred to as the *"ATIS"*.

| ATIS | SUNSHINE COAST | 114.2(2) 119.8(3) |

Notice there are two (2) frequencies. This allows the ATIS to be heard on both a discrete VHF frequency (119.8) and the VOR frequency (114.2). The crew can choose which one they want to listen to.

The ATIS is a recorded message that gives the crew important information in helping them to plan a take-off and a landing and is particularly important when making an instrument approach.

When tuned in to the correct frequency, the message runs continuously over and over again.

The ATIS is updated by the Tower controllers, who can read this information on an information panel at their desk (Figure 2). This information is received from meteorological instruments located at the airport, so it is an accurate report on conditions confirmed by people at the airfield.

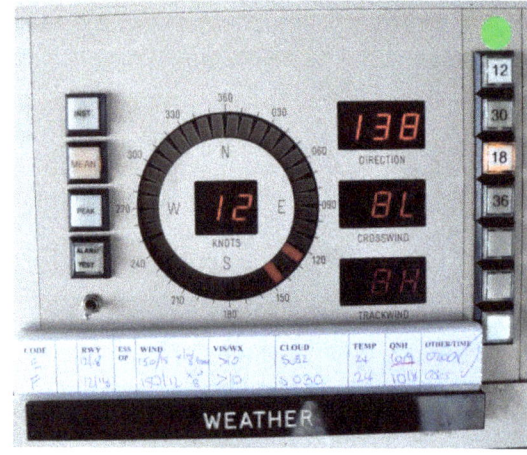

Figure 2 Panel in the tower showing the ATIS information

If the conditions change, the ATIS is updated. Each new ATIS message has a letter assigned to let aircrew know there has been a change.

The first ATIS recording of the day will be called Information ALPHA. On first contact with ATC, you must say that you have received information ALPHA, so they know you have all the information you need to take off and land. This also means that ATC does not have to tell you all of the information as you already have it.

When the message is changed, it will be given a new designator in order of the alphabet. For example, the first change to the ATIS will be designated BRAVO, and if it changes again it will be designated CHARLIE, and so on throughout the day.

If for some reason you cannot receive the ATIS information, then on first contact with Ground or Tower, say the words "Negative Information". This prompts the Ground or Tower controller to read you the ATIS information themselves as part of their call back to you.

When listening to the ATIS, it is important to write it down so you can refer to it later, when required.

The ATIS includes the following information:

Item	Description
The designator as a letter (A, B, C, etc.)	This indicates the recency of the ATIS
The runway in use	This is known as the duty runway direction
Wind direction and strength	Given as a compass bearing the wind is blowing from and its strength in knots
Cloud and visibility	Cloud amounts and heights above the ground, as well as the current visibility
OAT	The outside air temperature
QNH	The aerodrome QNH so that the altimeter will be accurate

Aerodrome Weather Information: AWIS or AWIB

The Aerodrome Weather Information Service (AWIS) or Aerodrome Weather Information Broadcast (AWIB) frequency can be found in ERSA and is referred to as *"AWIS" or "AWIB"*. (Both describe the same thing).

AWIS - 386 and 127.05, and Phone 07 4534 8828.

The AWIS can be received on multiple frequencies, depending on how the aerodrome operator has set it up and specific for a particular aerodrome.

The AWIS given above is for Toowoomba. It is available on the NDB frequency, VHF 127.05 and also available by phone. Interestingly, when the AWIS is provided over the phone it is given another name; it becomes a Weather and Terminal Information Reciter (*WATIR*). This is simply due to the technology used to make the system work.

The AWIS is very similar to the ATIS in that it is a recorded message that constantly repeats itself. The key difference is that it is not a recording of a report given by a Tower controller and does have a designator change when it is updated.

Instead, it is a computer-generated report based on meteorological instruments installed on the ground and interfacing with a computer. This combination of equipment is called an Automated Weather Station (AWS).

It provides varying information, depending on the sophistication (budget) of the aerodrome operator, but usually includes the station identifier (e.g. Toowoomba AWS aerodrome weather), wind in degrees magnetic and speed in knots, QNH, temperature in Celsius, cloud below 12,500 feet, visibility, dew point, humidity and rainfall in the last 10 minutes.

Although it repeats itself, it constantly updates the information every time it cycles through the information. If you listen to it once, then listen to it again, there may be differences, so it is considered "real-time" information and may be used by aircraft for instrument approaches.

The key advantage of AWIS is it operates 24/7.

Mike Becker, Becker Helicopters

Automatic Enroute Information Service (AERIS)

The Automatic Enroute Information Service (AERIS) frequency is found in green boxes printed on VTC, VNC, ERC, TAC and PCA.

The AERIS is designed to operate for aircraft above 5000 feet. If below 5000 feet, it may not be able to be received.

It is a repeated recording of METARS (Meteorological Terminal Aerodrome Reports) for major airports within the Meteorological AREA (see PCA [Planning Chart Australia]) you are flying in. This means it can be a very long message and may take 5-10 minutes to cycle through. It has limited use for DAY VFR helicopter operations but can be quite handy for IFR and long-range aircraft to get updated aerodrome information enroute without contacting Centre.

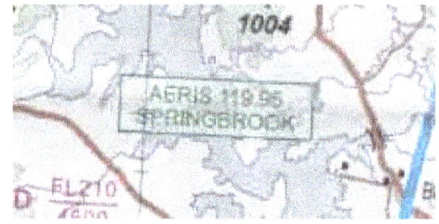

Figure 3 AERIS frequency printed on a chart

Airways Clearance Delivery (ACD)

The Airways Clearance Delivery (ACD) frequency can be found in ERSA and is referred to as *"{NAME} Delivery"*.

Example
For example, Brisbane Delivery
ACD   BRISBANE DELIVERY   118.6

Not all controlled airports have an ACD as they are only required at busy airports.

When used, you can directly contact the ACD controller responsible for giving you an airways clearance based on information received in your lodged flight plan. A flight plan must be submitted at least 30 minutes before making the initial call to ACD. If you do not lodge a flight plan, ACD will not give you clearance.

The ACD controller only needs to hear relevant information to issue a clearance; they do not need all the irrelevant information you give the Ground controller.

ACD need to know:

- your callsign
- the destination.

Everything else is already covered in the submitted flight plan.

Based on that, they give you either:

- the clearance you expect, or if they cannot do that, then
- an amended clearance that better suits their need to manage multiple aircraft trying to do the same thing.

The ACD controller is often sitting in a small room away from the tower. They cannot see outside but will have various screens and monitors and a keyboard that allows them to process airways clearances and flight plans. The ACD controller passes on the relevant information to the Ground Controller and the Tower Controller, who will then be expecting your calls.

Surface Movement Control (Ground) - SMC (Ground)

The Surface Movement Control (SMC) frequency can be found in the ERSA and it is referred to as *"{NAME} Ground"*.

Example
For example, Sunshine Coast Ground
SMC   SUNSHINE COAST   121.1

When used, you will be in direct contact with a Ground controller who is responsible for giving you instructions for taxiing *to* a helipad or a runway as well as taxi instructions *from* the helipad or runway back to your parking area after landing.

The ground controller needs to be given information that will help them to understand:

- where you are at the airport
- what sort of aircraft you are in
- how many people are on board
- if you have received the ATIS, and
- where you want to go to take off or if you have just landed, where you want to park.

If you give all of this information, he can look at all the other traffic and then give you a taxi clearance to get there.

The ground controller is often sitting in the tower at a separate station, either behind or below the tower controllers. They can talk directly to the tower controller to help improve the efficiency of any aircraft movements, so they know you are going to be calling them after landing. If there is an SMC controller, they have been informed by ACD that you have got a clearance and that you will be calling Ground shortly.

Figure 4 Ground Controller

At some airports that are not very busy, the SMC controller will do two jobs. They will control aircraft on the ground when outside the active Helipads or runways, but they can also issue Airways Clearances for those aircraft that need an airways clearance.

If there is no ACD, then the ground controller may be the first controller you call and they may give you an airways clearance.

Tower Controller

The Tower frequency can be found in the ERSA and is referred to as *"{NAME} Tower"*.

Example
For example, Sunshine Coast Tower
TWR   SUNSHINE COAST TOWER   (4)   124.4

Mike Becker, Becker Helicopters

When used, you will be in direct contact with the Tower controller who is responsible for issuing take-off and landing clearances, as well as controlling any aircraft that is within their Control Zone. They can issue, amend or change clearances based on the situation and have the ultimate control of managing traffic in and around the airport as soon as the aircraft is entering the active Helipad or runway.

Regardless of what the Ground controller or the ACD controller has given you, the Tower will have the overriding say, and you are not allowed to take-off or land without their permission.

The Tower controller sits inside the Control Tower and can usually see 360 degrees and view all runways, taxiways and helipads. They have access to computer screens and communication equipment so they can talk to aircraft and all the other ATC services and act as a hub for real-time information.

Figure 5 Sunshine Coast Control Tower

Departures and Approach

The Departures and Approach frequencies can be found in ERSA and are referred to as *"{NAME} Approach"* or *"{NAME} Departures"*.

> **Example**
>
> For example, Brisbane Approach or Brisbane Departures
>
> ```
> APP      BRISBANE APPROACH       124.7(2)  125.6(3)
> APP/DEP  BRISBANE APPROACH       123.5(4)
> DEP      BRISBANE DEPARTURES     118.45(3) 128.3(5)
> ```

Aviation Communication and Flight Radio *for Helicopter Pilots*

When used, you will be in direct contact with either the Approach or the Departures controller, who is responsible for managing all the conflicting traffic as they converge and diverge to and from an airport and cross each other going in different directions. This is probably the most stressful part of being an Air Traffic Controller as you cannot physically see any of these aircraft.

(FAA.gov, 2017 [cropped])

Instead, the Air Traffic Controller is positioned in a secured closed room with multiple screens showing data as it arrives. This data will come in the form of radar transmissions received from the aircraft's transponder, radio calls from the pilots, and other information passed onto them by the Tower controller or the ACD controller.

Additionally, a particular controller will be given a piece of airspace they have to manage. This means they will also be getting information from other approach and departure controllers who will be handing over aircraft as the aircraft leaves their piece of airspace and then moves into another piece of airspace.

When a pilot then comes on the radio not knowing what to say, or they go into someone's piece of airspace without permission, it can be a very frustrating and dangerous situation.

Not all airports have an Approach or Departures service. This is only needed for very busy airports where there are many aircraft coming in for a landing and taking off for a departure all at the same time.

The image below shows worldwide flights showing regions where high IFR aircraft congestion occurs.

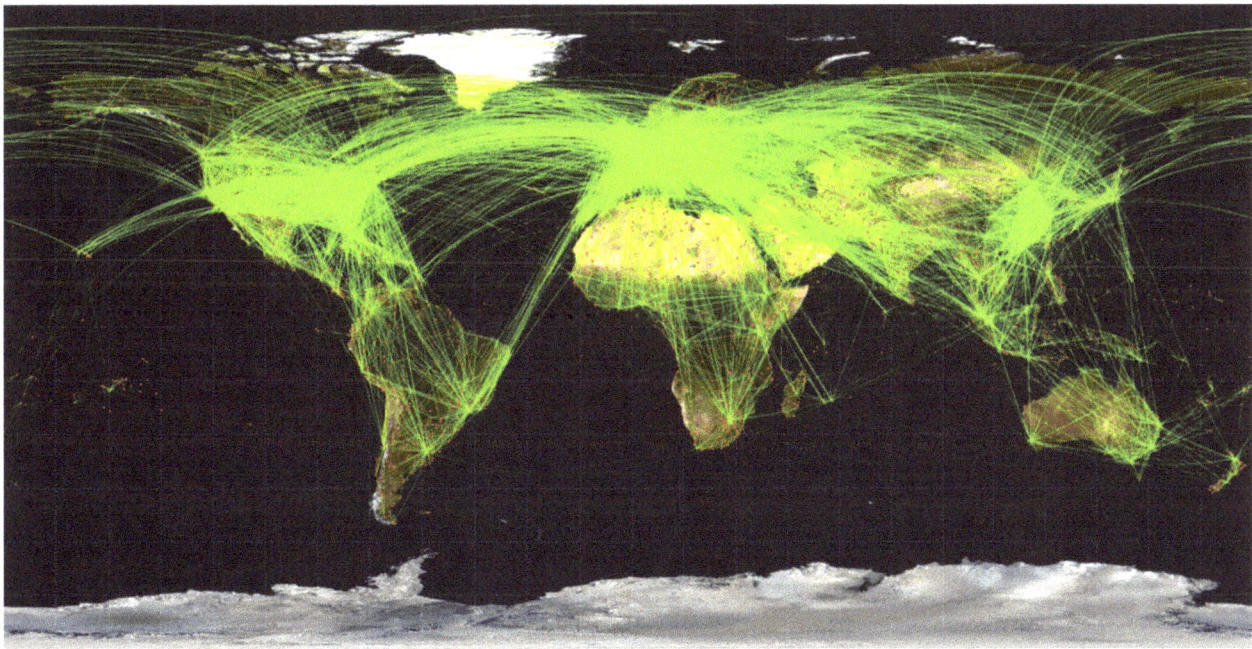

(Jpatokal, 2009)

Flight Information Area (FIA)

The Flight Information Area frequency can be found in several places. It can be found in the ERSA, on the VTC, VNC, ERC, TAC and PCA.

The Flight Information Area is referred to as *"{NAME} Centre"*.

Example
For example, Brisbane Centre FIA   BRISBANE CENTRE   125.7(6) 

Once the aircraft leaves the busy terminal area of an airport, it will be handed over to the Flight Information Area (FIA) controller (referred to as Centre), who can then manage the aircraft while it is cruising. If the aircraft is outside controlled airspace and is not IFR, it no longer needs to communicate to ATC but can maintain a listening watch and only make a broadcast if the pilot thinks it is necessary.

IFR aircraft are always followed by ATC, so regardless of being in controlled airspace or outside of it, they are required to still listen and make reports to ATC while in the cruise.

The FIA controller (Centre) needs varying information depending on the aircraft's operation (VFR, IFR, NVFR, NVG) and cruising level.

If operating VFR at lower levels outside controlled airspace, then there is no real requirement to talk to ATC unless necessary to request information, traffic conflicts, weather updates or a change in the flight plan.

If operating IFR, then ATC will constantly be monitoring you, and there will be a requirement to make reports at designated intervals or locations.

The FIA controller is similar to the Approach and Departure controller in that they are sitting in a secured room and cannot see the aircraft. Typically, they deal with fewer aircraft, so the stress levels are lower.

They still require accurate information which comes from:

- radar transmissions received from the aircraft's transponder, if within range
- radio calls from the pilots, and
- other information is passed onto them by the Tower controller, the ACD controller or another FIA controller that is passing on information about an aircraft that is just leaving their area and coming into the new area.

Flight Information Service (FIS)

The Flight Information Service (FIS) is provided on the FIA (Centre) frequency. It simply refers to a service the FIA controllers can provide to pilots while in flight if requested. It also allows pilots to pass on any relevant information they deem important for flight safety to the FIA controller, who in turn can pass on that information to other aircraft.

When communicating to the FIA controller to give or obtain flight information, the generic term **"Flightwatch"** is used.

Using the word **"Flightwatch"** allows the FIA controller to put a low priority on the request and they may come back and tell you to wait while they look after other aircraft that are making position and airways clearance calls, then come back to attend to your Flightwatch request.

> **Example**
>
> If cruising in the Brisbane FIR and wanting to amend a flight plan and obtain updated weather, the pilot would call
>
> ***"Brisbane Centre Flightwatch, request flight plan amendment and updated weather".***
>
> The FIA controller will then respond to this request as applicable.

Pilots can ask for the following information from the FIA controller:

- updated weather and NOTAMs (including VOLMET, turbulence, etc.)
- amend a flight plan
- cancel or activate a SARTIME
- make a phone call to the Company or destination if required
- any other aviation or inflight related request, which may include safety issues such as flocks of birds, dust storms, etc.

If the FIA controller gives out any information to aircraft, whether this is to individual aircraft or as a general broadcast to all aircraft, this is deemed to be a Flight Information Service.

Unicom

At some smaller airports, the local Council or a local group of aviation companies have received permission from CASA to operate their own radio frequency and have a person who can give relevant information to aircraft taking off and landing at that aerodrome.

The Unicom operator does not hold ATC qualifications but has done some training to use a radio. They cannot provide traffic separation or information, they cannot issue clearances, but they can give weather and local NOTAM information and make suggestions on where aircraft can land and park. This is a localised service with minimal support.

Outside controlled airspace (OCTA)

Outside controlled airspace (OCTA), there is no requirement to make a radio call unless you are within 10NM of an aerodrome or you want to broadcast on the Area frequency just to alert any local traffic where you are. It is up to aircrew to see and be seen and manage themselves.

Non-towered aerodromes

Aerodromes that are outside controlled airspace and do not have towers are called Non-towered Aerodromes and Common Traffic Advisory Frequency (CTAF) procedures apply. The aerodromes will be referred to as ***"{NAME} CTAF"***. For example, Gympie CTAF.

CTAF procedures refer to the specific radio calls that are required at designated positions when approaching, departing or transiting within 10NM of an aerodrome that does not have an active Tower controller. This means all aircraft will be saying and hearing the same things.

There are three (3) types of non-towered aerodromes, they are:

1. **Certified** (CERT) aerodromes
2. **Uncertified** (UNCR) aerodromes and
3. **Registered** (REG) aerodromes

Certified aerodrome

A Certified Aerodrome is an aerodrome that has been certified by CASA and often has either an RPT (Regular Public Transport) service or an instrument approach procedure at the aerodrome. At certified aerodromes, it is mandatory that all aircraft have a VHF radio and that they are used to apply the CTAF procedures.

To know if an aerodrome is certified, refer to the ERSA, and it will state CERT just below the aerodrome identifier.

You may find some aerodromes in the ERSA have the designator REG (Registered). This is an older version and has the same meaning as Certified, but the document has not yet been updated.

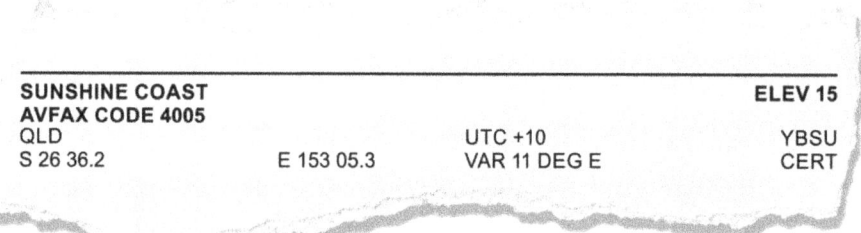

Un-certified aerodrome

An Uncertified Aerodrome is an aerodrome that has *not* been certified by CASA and often does not have either an RPT (Regular Public Transport) service or an instrument approach procedure at the aerodrome. At uncertified aerodromes, it is *not* mandatory that all aircraft have a VHF radio, which means that there may be some private aircraft flying in the vicinity of the aerodrome or conducting circuits that do not have any form of radio communication.

If the aircraft does have a radio, then it must be used applying the CTAF procedures.

Un-certified aerodromes are identified in the ERSA; they are shaded and have UNCR just under the aerodrome identifier.

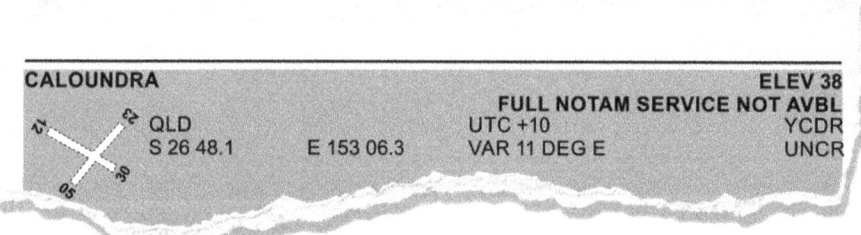

Registered aerodrome

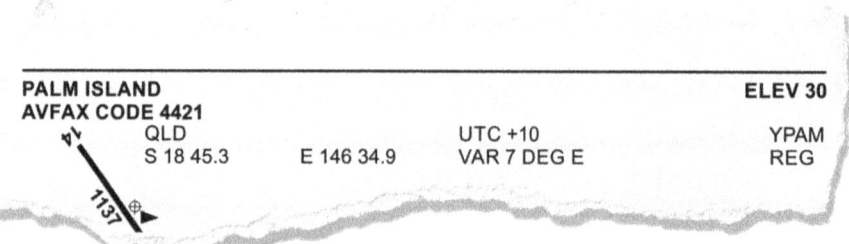

Standard CTAF procedures

The standard recommended CTAF radio calls at a non-towered aerodrome are as follows:

- **Inbound** before reaching 10NM from the aerodrome stating position, height and intentions with an ETA for the circuit area.
- **Joining** the circuit within 3NM of the runway with a description of which part of the circuit you are joining and landing details.
- **Overhead** if conducting a standard overhead re-join procedure

Additional calls may include:

- **Downwind** with landing details
- **Base;** and/or
- **Finals**

The following final four (4) calls are only recommended if the pilot thinks it is necessary to assist other traffic in maintaining separation. If there are no other aircraft in the vicinity or there are too many pilots on the radio, then do not make these calls.

- Vacating the helipad or runway and taxing to parking
- Taxing to the helipad or runway in preparation for a take-off
- A take-off call and in what direction with your intentions; and
- A departure call.

Remember, the premise of making radio calls is to ensure safety and help other aircraft know who and where you are. If there are no other aircraft or if the other aircraft already know who and where you are and what you are doing, then do not clutter up the radio with unnecessary radio calls.

> **Example**
>
> Consider approaching Gympie Airport at 1500 with the intention of landing. The sequence of the radio calls may be similar to the following:
>
> *"Gympie traffic, Helicopter WCF Bell 206 is 12NM to the east of the field at 1500 inbound, estimate the circuit 15, Gympie."*
>
> *"All stations Gympie, Helicopter WCF Bell206 is the circuit area at 1000 joining downwind runway 14 for a landing direct to the centre windsock, Gympie."*
>
> *"WCF is clear of the runway, Gympie."*

Tower Operating Hours

Some towered aerodromes in both Class C and D airspace will only have certain operating hours. This means when the tower is closed, CTAF procedures apply and they are treated in the same manner as a licenced non-towered aerodrome.

Most Military aerodromes operate like this, as do most towers located in Class D airspace.

Example
The Sunshine Coast aerodrome is an example of this.
TWR HR - 2130-0940 UTC daily. Phone 07 5448 7662^. TWR HR may change at short notice, check status of airspace with ATS or Sunshine Coast ATIS. Sunshine Coasts TWR provides combined TWR & APP CTL services within Class D airspace 4500FT AMSL & BLW DRG TWR HR. CTC TWR for clearance. Outside TWR HR, Sunshine Coast Class D airspace 4500FT AMSL & BLW becomes Class G. Brisbane Centre 123.0 operates Sunshine Coast Class C airspace DRG TWR HR. FIA on ground COMS may be available with ATS dependent on ACFT location and building shielding.

To determine if an aerodrome tower will be operating before the flight, consult the ERSA or NOTAM.

Summary of Who to Call

It is up to the crew to determine *"Who"* they need to talk to.

Good knowledge of where to find the appropriate radio frequencies is important.

Prior preparation before a flight and writing down the radio frequencies on your kneeboard or map will go a long way to ensuring a successful flight.

When to call

ATIS

Before contacting any ATC unit, the pilot shall obtain the ATIS or AWIS, if it is available.

Airways Clearance Delivery (ACD)

At an aerodrome that has an Airways Clearance Delivery (ACD), contact them before calling ground and ask for the Airways Clearance. ACD will give the clearance, which needs to be written down and read back so that the controller knows you have heard it correctly. At large busy airports, this may even be done before starting the engine.

While in-flight and coming into a large aerodrome that has ACD, there is no requirement to call them before entering. Instead, it is mandatory that a flight plan be lodged and, therefore, they will already know you are coming. If, for some reason, you have to enter controlled airspace and there is no flight plan in the system, then, in the first instance, call the FIA controller and ask them to put details in the system for you as part of the Flight Information Service (FIS). Civil ACD controllers will not talk to aircraft once they are in the air.

At all Military aerodromes, it is a requirement that incoming aircraft call ACD while in flight before entering the Control Zone (CTR) or Control Area (CTA). This is an additional requirement when compared to a civil aerodrome and is an area that can cause confusion. Military ACD controllers *will* talk to aircraft while in flight and *will* give clearances while in flight.

SMC (Surface Movement Control) referred to as Ground (GND)

If you are at an aerodrome that requires permission to start the engine (refer to ERSA or NOTAM), the crew can contact Ground and request an engine start. This is important when the controllers are trying to manage multiple aircraft in and out of the aerodrome at the same time. If there are going to be delays, it is better not to be burning fuel you had planned on for the flight while sitting on the ground.

If there is no requirement to request an engine start, then go through all the run-up procedures. Once completed, then call Ground and ask for a taxi clearance to the take-off area.

If you are at a smaller aerodrome, then ACD and Ground may be combined and you will do both ACD and the Ground calls on the same frequency at the same time to the same Ground controller.

Tower (TWR)

After taxing to the take-off helipad or runway holding point and you are ready for the take-off, you may call the tower and tell them that you are **"Ready"**.

"Ready" is the standard word used to tell the Tower controller that all checks have been done and the aircraft is ready for take-off.

At that point, the Tower controller will either:

- tell you to wait as other traffic takes-off and lands in front of you, or
- give you a clearance to enter the active helipad or runway and then "take off" with any additional instructions that may be required, such as turn left or right, etc.

Departures and Approach

After take-off and while still within the control zone, you will remain on the Tower frequency until you are told to go to another frequency by the Tower controller. Whenever you are in controlled airspace, you will be told what to do, so do not worry too much about what comes next.

At smaller Towered aerodromes, the Approach and Departure controller is the Tower controller, so there will be no frequency change.

At large Class C aerodromes, the Tower controller will hand you over to the Departures Controller on departure.

When coming into a large Class C aerodrome, the Flight Information Area controller will hand you over to an Approach Controller, who in turn will hand you over to the Tower before landing.

The important thing to remember here is you will be told what to do and you will be given the frequency, so much of the mental stress is managed for you.

Approach and Departure controllers will have you on their radar screens, they will know your position over the ground, they will also know your height; however, because the transponder can fail they will constantly ask you to confirm your height so they can cross-check it with their radar.

All an Approach and Departure controller needs to hear is your callsign, the height you are currently at and the height you are descending or climbing to.

Flight Information Area (FIA)

Once you leave the terminal area of the aerodrome, which is typically 30 NM from the Runway, the Departures controller will hand you over to the Flight Information Area (FIA) controller (Centre).

If on approach into the aerodrome, at approximately 30 NM the FIA controller (Centre) will hand you over to the Approach controller.

If you are remaining inside controlled airspace, the FIA controller will monitor your progress and you will be required to make regular reports.

If you leave controlled airspace, the FIA controller will tell you that the Radar services are terminated and you can then be responsible for yourself and do as you please with no requirement to make any further radio calls (unless the flight is IFR).

Unicom

A Unicom aerodrome is to be treated the same as a non-towered aerodrome, but when you make the CTAF call, a Unicom operator will respond with any relevant information and a suggestion on where to land. You can respond in plain English, as required.

Non-towered aerodrome

Before reaching 10NM from a non-towered aerodrome, the pilot shall call on the designated CTAF frequency. If the aerodrome does not have a designated frequency, which can be found in ERSA, then the standard frequency of 126.7 is to be used. This is referred to as the *"Multicomm"* frequency.

The rule is that the call shall be made "BY" 10NM, which means it can be made much sooner depending on the performance of the aircraft. In general, pilots should consider making a call when approaching within 15NM of a non-towered aerodrome to allow for other traffic, radio chatter and better planning and preparation for circuit entry.

How to call

Although making a radio call seems very simple, when you do it for the first time, you will find that your mind goes blank and you do not know what to say.

To fix this, we suggest writing the calls down on paper for the first few times. Practice them in the classroom with other trainees. Rehearse the entire flight, and rehearse making radio calls. Listen to the radio on the ground and get used to the words that you will say and how to say them.

Practice, Practice, Practice

Techniques when making a call

Speak Slowly

When speaking on a radio, make a conscious effort to speak slower than normal. It can be difficult to hear on the radio, so if the pilot transmitting is speaking very quickly, the words can get confused and merge together into just one big continuous amount of noise.

If the radio call is being written down, then pause between sentences and pause between each word or number. It is much better to make one radio call slowly than have to repeat it several times because you are saying it so fast that it cannot be understood.

Articulate your words

Make a conscious effort to pronounce the words clearly. Non-native English speakers will have difficulty in both transmitting and receiving radio calls, simply because of the enunciation (the way words are pronounced or spoken). Practice the words you will use. Say them slowly. Say each syllable, if necessary, or even change the word to use a simpler word that means the same thing.

Avoid words like Ummmm, Arrrr, Mmmmm, Aye, etc.

If you forget what to say, then release the transmit button. Do not keep holding in the transmit key while saying nothing having long pauses and, therefore, preventing other aircraft from making radio calls.

Volume

When speaking, try not to shout, but also do not speak too quietly. You need to project your voice into the microphone, rather than talking in the back of your throat and try to speak at an even volume.

Speak into the microphone

The microphone attached to a helmet or headset is omni-directional and very sensitive. Because the manufacturer knows that it will be used in a very noisy environment, it is made so that it does not pick up outside noises easily. It is very important that it is positioned within 1 centimetre of your mouth. If it is further away than that, then the microphone will struggle to pick up the vibrations from your voice and translate them into an electrical signal that can be used.

Listen

Listening is a skill that needs to be learned. Being able to hear radio calls and understand what is being said takes listening skills. Focus on the radio call and avoid thinking about your reply until you have fully understood what has been said. Do not hesitate in asking for the transmission to be repeated if you did not understand any part of it.

Broadcasts

When outside controlled airspace, pilots are required to make *"Broadcasts"*.

A broadcast is a general call given to inform anyone that is listening. It is not directly made to a specific aircraft, station or ATC.

Broadcasts can be divided into two categories

1. Calls made to no specific *station* outside the circuit area (greater than 3 NM) of an aerodrome and prefixed by the words *"All Stations XYZ"*
2. Calls made to *traffic* within the circuit area (within 3 NM) of an aerodrome and prefixed by the words *"XYZ Traffic"*

Example of a radio broadcast away from the circuit
"All stations Noosa, Helicopter WCF a Bell 206 Jet Ranger, 5 NM to the west of the field at 1500 feet, tracking coastal northbound for Rainbow Beach. All stations Noosa."

Example of a radio broadcast within the circuit area
"Noosa Traffic, Helicopter WCF, downwind runway 27 for a landing at the centre windsock, Noosa Traffic."

Report

When having to maintain contact with a particular ATC unit, either inside or outside controlled airspace, pilots are required to make *"Reports"*.

Reports are made to specific ATC units at specific times and/or places and contain specific information that is usually expected.

Example
"Brisbane Centre, WCF maintaining 6500 estimate Kingaroy at 05"

Calls

When communicating with a specific station, whether that be an ATC unit, another aircraft or another station on the ground to exchange information, this is referred to as a *"Call"*.

Example
"Gympie Traffic and Ultralight 445, Helicopter WCF Bell 206 is downwind runway 14 touch and go Gympie"

Aviation Communication and Flight Radio *for Helicopter Pilots*

What to say

Radio calls have standard information and can be reasonably predictable. If the following questions are answered, then you will make the perfect radio call every time.

Question	Memory jogger
What frequencies are required?	**Radio**
Who am I calling?	**Station called**
Who am I?	**Station calling**
Where am I?	**Position**
What is my height?	**Height**
What do I want to do?	**Intentions**
Will I need a clearance?	**Clearance**

The standard pattern of the radio call, therefore, typically follows the same flow as listed below:

1. Radio
2. Station called
3. Station calling
4. Position
5. Height
6. Intentions
7. Clearance

If this short list of information is memorised and then written on a kneepad, it will act as a memory jogger to help you find and say the correct information when making a radio call.

Example	

On a flight from Kingaroy to the Sunshine Coast, which is a Towered Class D aerodrome, at 1500 feet and currently 15 NM from the Sunshine Coast the radio call may be put together as follows:

Memory jogger	Answer
Radio	ATIS 119.8 (listen to it now and get the designator) Tower 124.4 set on the VHF radio
Station called	Sunshine Coast Tower
Station calling	Helicopter WCF a Bell206
Position	15 NM to the west of the airfield
Height	1500 feet
Intentions	Track inbound for a landing on Pad Delta
Clearance	Yes

The radio call would, therefore, be:

"Sunshine Coast Tower, Helicopter WCF a Bell 206, Received Information Alpha, 15NM to the West of the field at 1500 feet, inbound for a landing at Pad Delta, Request Airways Clearance."

Radio calls do not have to be any more complicated than this. Instead, they will just vary in the content and will get easier the more you practice them.

Aviation Communication and Flight Radio *for Helicopter Pilots*

The following is a step by step guide to making a radio call.

Step	Action	Discussion
1	Determine your position	Check against the map and GPS and determine where you are and when your next radio call will be.
2	Determine the frequency to use	Look at the Frequency boundary change lines and the Frequency boxes. Look at the aerodromes close to you. Check the ERSA. Much of this can be done in the planning stages of the flight, so there should be no surprises.
3	Enter the frequency in the radio	Using the VHF radio you want to transmit on, use the selector knobs to dial up the correct frequency.
4	Audio panel selection	Select the correct radio to listen to and the correct radio to transmit on by selecting the buttons and knobs on the Audio Panel.
5	Volume	Check that the volume is adjusted correctly. If necessary pull/push the squelch button to the OFF position to hear the background noise volume and then adjust the volume control on the radio and/or headset as required. Then push/pull the squelch back to the ON position.
6	Listen	Listen to the radio for at least 30 seconds to ensure that you are not going to make a transmission over someone else who is also on the radio at the same time. If someone else is talking, then do not transmit, but listen to what they are saying.
7	Think	Think about what you are going to say. Use the memory joggers to help compose the call. Radio	Stations	Position	Height	Intentions	Airways Clearance If necessary, write it down, so that you know what you are going to say and to whom.
8	Transmit	When ready, pull the transmit trigger on the cyclic. Do not speak for the first 2 seconds; instead, look at the VHF radio where you should see either a TX or a T appear on the radio that you want to use. If the TX or T does not display, then release the trigger and repeat Step 4 as you may be on the wrong radio. If the TX or T displays, then you are transmitting on the correct radio and you may now make the radio call. Speak clearly and slowly.
9	Receive	Once you have finished making the call, release the transmit trigger and wait for a response. You may be expected to read back some of the information in the call, so, if possible, be ready with a pen and paper to write it down, instead of trying to remember it.

Readback

There will be times when parts of the radio call received from ATC will have to be read back, so that they know you have received and understood the message in the radio call properly.

A readback takes practice as you have to be able to hear what is being said to you, usually very quickly, through radio static, and with lots of external noise, then repeat it back (Readback).

Multi-crew operations have an advantage that while one pilot can fly, the other can work the radio and can write down (in shorthand) the radio call so that they know what to read back.

Single pilot operations become more difficult, particularly in a helicopter when you cannot let go of the controls, so the pilot will rely on memory for the read back.

If you do not get the entire message the first time or are having trouble understanding the controller, do not hesitate in asking for the message to be said again or even ask the controller to speak slower.

Example

Consider a call given by the Sunshine Coast Ground controller that you did not hear properly, you may reply:

"Sunshine Coast ground WCF say again"

This will be the radio call you make so that the controller says the entire radio message again.

Another example is if the controller is speaking too fast and you could not understand because of the speed of the message. In this instance, you may say

"Sunshine Coast Ground, WCF, please say again, slower"

There may be many examples of what you could say back to the controller. The point is, if you do not understand a call, have it repeated until you do and can then read it back correctly.

In essence, if you are familiar with the radio calls, you will usually only receive expected radio calls and all the information should be predictable.

Memorising a readback is a skill that has to be repeated and practised.

The following information is required to be read back:

- Take-off and landing instructions
- Transponder codes
- Any height limits given
- Any clearance limit (that is a height or distance restriction)
- Any heading and speed instructions
- QNH settings
- Frequency changes; and
- Taxi, backtracking or runway crossing instructions.

Over Transmissions

"Over Transmissions" is when you make a radio call at the same time another aircraft is also trying to make a radio call on the same frequency. Unfortunately, both transmitting aircraft will never know they have over transmitted each other unless a third aircraft comes on the radio and tells them.

The danger is that both aircraft needed to hear what the other was saying for separation purposes, but now neither of them knows the other exists.

To help avoid over transmitting, when first changing frequency, do not immediately transmit. Instead, it is good practice to spend at least a minute listening on the radio and gaining an understanding of who else is out there and who else is making radio calls.

If you hear two other aircraft over transmitting each other, the radio will make a loud squealing sound as both radio transmissions clash with each other.

If possible, you can come on the radio after they have made their calls and inform them that they were both transmitting at the same time, and if you know the callsign of either one, you can give that aircraft priority to try again.

> **Example**
>
> You receive two transmissions at once and cannot understand any of them. The transmission then ends. At that time, you can transmit and say the following:
>
> *"Two at once. WCU say again."*

Clipped Transmissions

A clipped transmission ends halfway through transmission. This is most common when the pilot accidentally lets go of the transmit trigger and does not realise it. The danger is only half the message was received.

If you receive a clipped transmission, you can go back to the other aircraft and ask them to say it all again. Additionally, if you were the aircraft that stopped transmitting, the aircraft you were trying to talk to may come back and ask you to say the whole or part of the transmission again.

> **Example**
>
> *"WCU say again all after position"*

Establish Comms

There will be times when you may need to first establish communication before making the full radio call. This may be due to poor radio reception, a busy traffic environment or a local aerodrome procedure.

It is a requirement to establish comms if entering Controlled airspace without a flight plan, as they will not be expecting you.

It is not a requirement to establish comms if you have lodged a flight plan and the controller knows you are coming.

To establish communication, it is as simple as calling on the frequency, addressing the station being called and letting them know you want to talk to them.

> **Example 1**
>
> *"Sunshine Coast Tower Helicopter WCF with inbound details"*
>
> The above radio call tells the Sunshine Coast Tower that you want to talk to them, and give them your full radio call asking for permission to come in for a landing.

> **Example 2**
>
> *"Sunshine Coast Tower Helicopter WCF with transit details"*
>
> The above radio call tells the Sunshine Coast Tower that you want to talk to them, and give them your full radio call asking for permission to transit through the zone while enroute to somewhere else and you will not be landing.

Example 3

"Sunshine Coast Tower Helicopter WCF with Airwork details"

The above radio call tells the Sunshine Coast Tower that you want to talk to them and give them your full radio call asking for permission to enter the zone and conduct some aerial work (such as photography), but you will not be landing. They will respond with:

"WCF, Sunshine Coast Tower, go ahead"

Once communication with ATC has been established, it is no longer a requirement to be stating their callsign on every call. Instead, the calls can be abbreviated with detail and the callsign of the aircraft only.

Courtesy Calls

There will be times when you may need to establish communication with a Tower controller or the ATC responsible for controlled airspace if you are going to be passing very close to the boundary, but not entering their airspace.

A courtesy call is not a mandatory requirement, and it is not documented anywhere, but it does display good airmanship and an understanding of what air traffic controllers need to manage their airspace and allows for the safe movement of aircraft in and around controlled airspace.

Consider the airspace in the image below, where a helicopter is transiting south along the motorway.

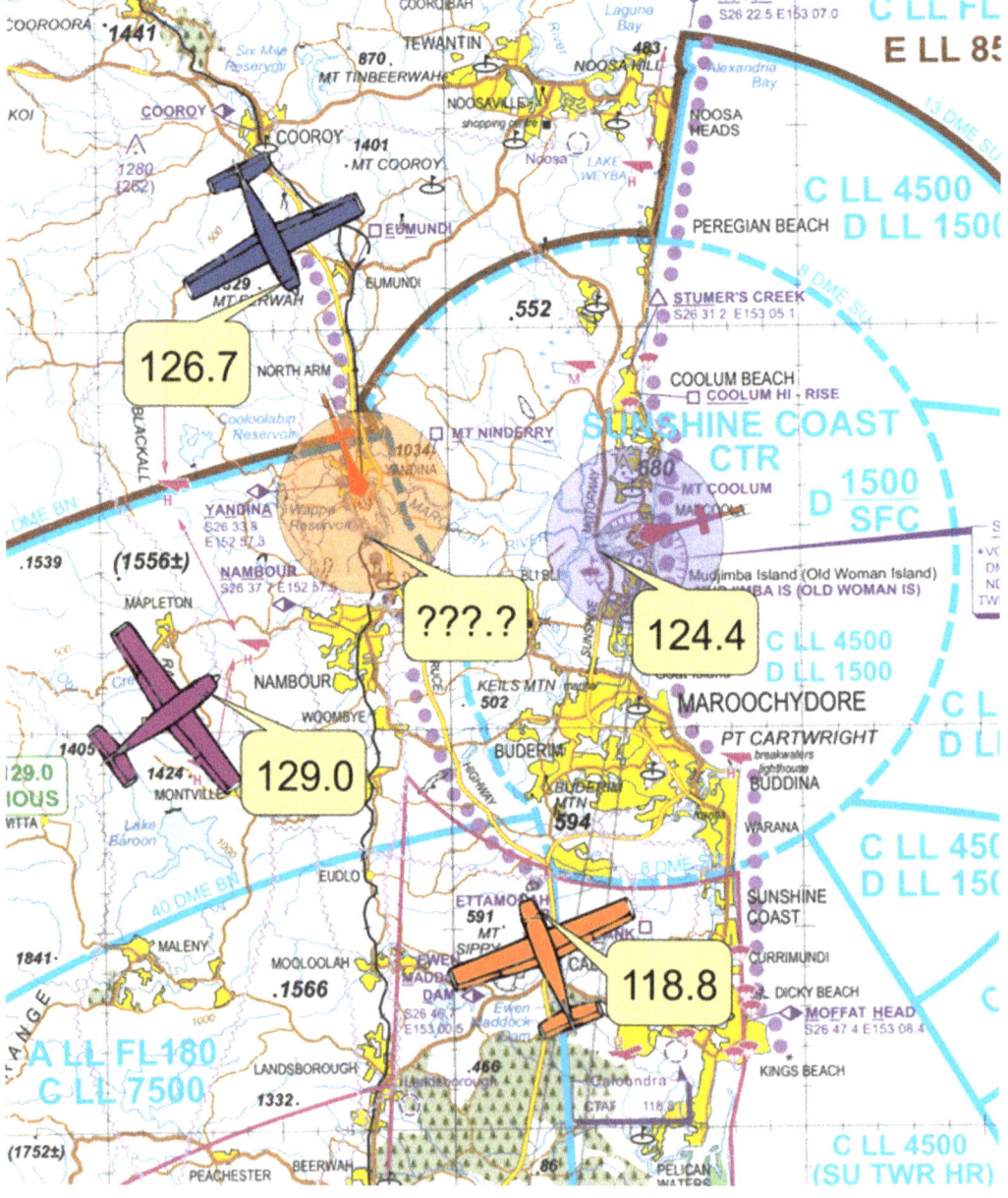

Aviation Communication and Flight Radio *for Helicopter Pilots*

Although the aircraft is outside of controlled airspace (OCTA), it is running very close to a CTR boundary. In this same airspace, you may have aircraft all legitimately on different frequencies as follows:

1. The Area frequency OCTA (in this case 129.0)
2. The Tower frequency (in this case 124.4)
3. The local CTAF frequency for non-towered aerodromes located both north and south of the CTR (in this case 118.8 and 126.7)

Having aircraft in close proximity on different frequencies can be a problem, so it is up to the pilot to decide which frequency is most appropriate to be listening and transmitting on, given the prevailing circumstances. There is no right or wrong answer here. Experience and local knowledge will help pilots make the most appropriate decision.

In the previous case, let's assume you are in an aircraft at 1500 feet tracking south along the Highway. Although you are outside controlled airspace and have no intention of entering it, you are flying within 2 NM of the airspace boundary and other aircraft may be entering or exiting the airspace right in front of you. Additionally, you may have other VFR aircraft OCTA tracking north along the highway in the opposite direction, avoiding controlled airspace just like you are.

If you have two (2) radios, good airmanship would dictate that you at least listen out on the Tower frequency as well as the Area frequency, so that you can hear other traffic. The problem is other traffic will not know you are there unless something is said on the radio.

In these cases, it is always good airmanship to make a "Courtesy Call" notifying the Tower on the Tower frequency and the Area on the Area frequency of your intentions and letting them know your position, height and intentions.

This way, the Tower can give you any conflicting traffic and also allows the Tower to pass on your details to other aircraft that you may conflict with.

This also notifies any other aircraft on the Area frequency of your location and intentions, and in turn, they may communicate with you telling you where they are.

The radio call to the Tower may be as follows:

> *"Sunshine Coast Tower, Helicopter WCF Bell206 with a courtesy call"*
>> *WCF, Sunshine Coast Tower, go ahead"*
>
> *"Helicopter WCF Bell 206 is over Yandina tracking south along the Bruce Highway at 1500 remaining OCTA"*
>> *"WCF, thank you, no known traffic"*
>
> *"WCF"*

The radio call on the Area frequency may be as follows:

> *"All stations in the Yandina area, Helicopter WCF Bell 206 is 1 NM south of Yandina at 1500 tracking south along the highway to Brisbane, All station in the Yandina area"*

Readability scale

The readability scale is a standard way for pilots and ATC controllers to communicate when asking each other the quality of their radio transmissions. The readability scale encompasses two items:

- **Readability**, that is how clear the signal is and how well you can understand what is being said.
- **Strength**, which is how strong the signal is. If it is a weak signal you may not be able to hear it all the way through, compared to a strong signal that you can hear very well.

The readability scale is divided into 5 categories as follows:

Scale	Readability of transmission	Strength of signal
1	Unreadable	Very weak
2	Partly readable	Poor
3	Readable with difficulty	Fair
4	Readable	Good
5	Perfect	Excellent

Readability scale format: single- or double-digit

The readability scale can be given as either a single number or as a double number. Which one is used depends on the preference of the person giving the feedback.

Using the single-digit method

When using the single-digit method, both the readability and the strength are rated as one unit as if they are both the same.

Example
A score of 5 means that the readability and the strength of the signal are both perfect.
A score of 3 means that the readability and the strength of the signal are both average. Readable, but with a bit of difficulty.

Using the double-digit method:

When using the double-digit method, the readability and the strength of the signal are rated individually and given separate numbers according to how they are received. In these instances, you will give both a readability and strength score.

Example
A score of 5 by 2 means that the readability is perfect, the words are coming through very clearly, but the signal strength is poor and the receiver is struggling to hear because they cannot get enough volume from the transmission.
A score of 1 by 5 means that the transmission is unreadable, no words can be understood, but the signal strength is strong and the receiver is getting a loud signal.

When to use the readability scale

The readability scale is used when:

- you want to check the readability of your transmission with another station, or
- the other station wants to check their readability with you.

It is commonly used by ATC when they have had difficulty communicating with an aircraft (often because the pilot turned the radio down and forgot), and they are establishing that your radio works correctly and that you are again receiving transmissions.

Example

The call on the radio may go something like this:
 	
"WCF, Sunshine Coast Tower, how are you reading this transmission"
    "Sunshine Coast Tower, WCF, reading you 5 by 5"
"WCF, Sunshine Coast Tower, Roger, reading you 2 please try second radio"
    "Sunshine Coast Tower, WCF on box (COMM) 2, how do you read now"
"WCF, Sunshine Coast Tower, reading you 5"

When the Radio Fails

Aim

This chapter aims to introduce the trainee to:

- troubleshooting radio failures, and
- radio failure procedures.

Related documents

- ERSA: Emergency Procedures, 1.5 Communication Failure

Introduction

When the radio fails, it is to be considered an inconvenience and not a major problem.

The aircraft will still fly normally; a safe landing is still assured; you simply cannot communicate your intentions via the radio.

Troubleshooting Radio Failure

The moment the radio fails, the first thing to do is troubleshoot the problem. Most of the time (90%), the radio has not failed, but the pilot or crew have pushed the wrong button, disconnected a headset or selected the wrong frequency.

The key to troubleshooting a radio failure is to start with the simplest and most obvious and then work to the more complicated and less obvious.

Item	Check
Circuit Breakers	IN
Radio	ON
Volume	UP (use the squelch to confirm)
Frequency	Correct
Audio panel	Correct COMM selected to Listen and Transmit Audio Panel Radio volume UP Microphone has not been isolated on the audio panel Check squelch All other settings correct
Voltage	Check that the voltage at the battery is sufficient. If less, then check the Generator is ON. Low voltage can lead to a radio failure.
Headset/Helmet	Plugged IN (check it is plugged in all the way). Volume UP. Other helmet and headset connections checked.
Swap radios	If the aircraft has two VHF radios then switch to the second radio.

Item	Check
Second Pilot and Crew	Check that all crew members have lost radio COMMs. It may be isolated to your helmet or pilot station only.
	If you are the only one with a failure, hand over the radios to the second pilot or swap helmets or headsets. If not, continue with the Radio Failure Procedures.
Crew resource management (CRM)	Communicate with the rest of the crew to come up with any other suggestions.
	If the radio/s have definitely failed, then revert to the Radio Failure Procedures.
Mobile phone	If there is a mobile phone on board and it can be easily used in flight, then it may be used as a radio if you can contact ATC by phone. Alternatively, it can be used to contact the Company who will contact ATC for you and come up with a plan for your return to the aerodrome.
ADF/VOR	If the aircraft has an ADF or VOR, listen out on those frequencies as ATC (if in a control zone) may be able to make a transmission on those frequencies for you to hear. This is not common, but it is possible to do.

Radio Failure Procedures

Once it is established that the:

- the radio system has failed, and
- the troubleshooting has not fixed the problem, and
- there is no communication with ATC or the Company,
  then remember to:

AVIATE | NAVIGATE | COMMUNICATE

Every situation can be different, so you may have to make decisions based on your current situation, but it is most important to remember to:

- keep flying the aircraft in a safe manner (Aviate)
- fly to an area where it is safe (Navigate), and then
- communicate (which cannot be done by radio at this time).

There are two standard responses; they are radio failure procedure:

- **inside** controlled airspace; or
- **outside** controlled airspace.

Radio Failure Inside Controlled Airspace

The following steps shall be followed after a Radio failure within controlled airspace.

	Action	Discussion
1	Transponder	SQUAWK 7600 (Need a fix)
2	Transmit	Transmit the message that you have a radio failure and state your intentions. The radio call shall be preceded by using the words **"Transmitting Blind"** This means that you have had a radio failure and cannot hear anything. The reason this is done is the radio may still be able to transmit, but you just do not know it. So continue to make calls anyway, just in case. *For example:* *"Sunshine Coast Tower, Helicopter WCF Transmitting Blind, Radio Failure, 5NM to the west of the field making a straight-in approach to Pad Juliet"*
3	VMC	If in VMC, remain in VMC (do not go into the cloud) and divert to the nearest suitable aerodrome making Transmitting Blind calls as you go. Use standard procedures and see and avoid techniques. Turn all lights and strobes ON.
4	IMC	If in IMC, or cannot maintain VMC (you are in the cloud) continue under the last ATC clearance you received and operate in accordance with your flight plan. Conduct an instrument approach with at least one holding pattern. Use standard procedures and see and avoid techniques. Turn all lights and strobes ON.
5	ATC	Upon landing, contact ATC by phone.

Radio Failure Outside of Controlled Airspace

The following steps shall be followed after a radio failure outside controlled airspace (OCTA).

	Action	Discussion
1	Transponder	SQUAWK 7600 (Need a fix)
2	Transmit	Transmit the message that you have a radio failure and state your intentions.
		The radio call shall be preceded by using the words **"Transmitting Blind."**
		This means that you have had a radio failure and cannot hear anything. The reason this is done is the radio may still be able to transmit, but you just do not know it. So continue to make calls anyway, just in case.
		For example:
		"All Stations Gympie, Helicopter WCF Transmitting Blind, Radio Failure, 5NM to the west of the field joining left base runway 32 Gympie."
3	VMC	If in VMC, remain in VMC (do not go into the cloud) and divert to the nearest suitable aerodrome making Transmitting Blind calls as you go.
		Do not enter Controlled Airspace; divert to avoid it.
		Use standard procedures and see and avoid techniques.
		Turn all lights and strobes ON.
4	IMC	If in IMC or cannot maintain VMC (you are in the cloud), continue under the last ATC clearance you received and operate in accordance with your flight plan.
		Assuming operations under the IFR, then continue on the flight plan and enter controlled airspace, if necessary.
		Conduct an instrument approach with at least one holding pattern.
		Use standard procedures and see and avoid techniques.
		Turn all lights and strobes ON.
		Consult the ERSA for more detailed instructions.
5	ATC	Upon landing, contact ATC by phone.

Light Signals

The following light signals may be used by the Tower to communicate with aircraft that have a radio failure.

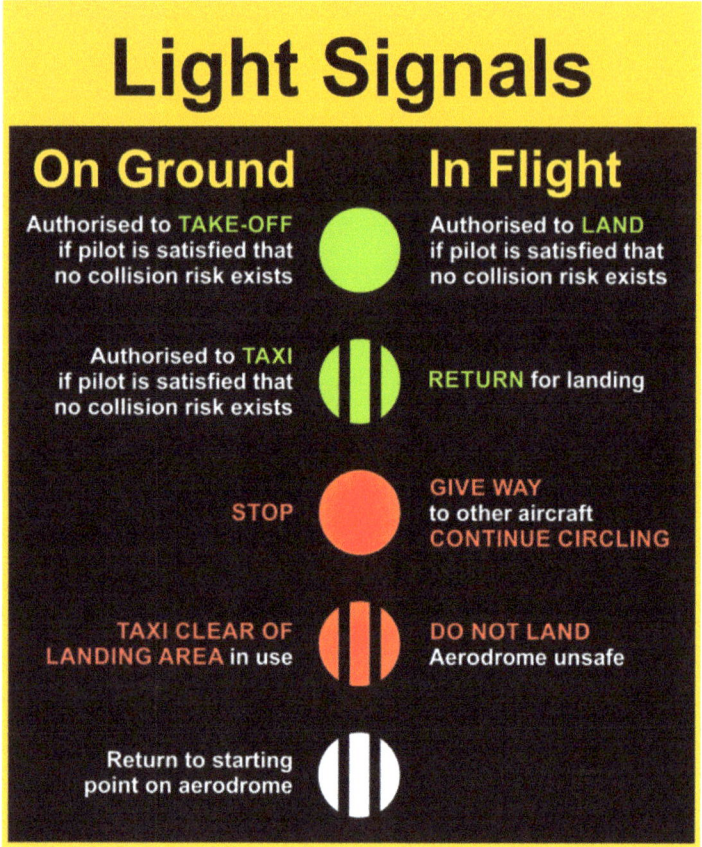

The light signals are given by the controller in the Tower, who has access to a high powered light that they can direct at the aircraft, and the controller will then pull a trigger on the light to activate it in the desired sequence.

White	Green	Red

Local Procedures

Most operators will have some local radio failure procedures that apply to operations at their base airfield.

These procedures will be stated in a company's Operations Manual and company pilots should be familiar with these.

Distress and Emergency Calls

Aim

This chapter aims to:

- Introduce the trainee to Distress and Urgency radio calls.

Related documents

- Aviation Law course notes
- ERSA Emergencies
- AIP

Introduction to Distress and Emergency Calls

At some time during your flying career, you will encounter a situation where you, the aircraft or someone else is either in DISTRESS or is in an URGENT situation. In these circumstances, aviators follow the rule:

CANCA:

Communicate | Aviate | Navigate | Communicate | Administrate

C	Communicate	**Communicate internally** by announcing what the emergency is to the crew.
A	Aviate	**Aviate** simply means that your priority is to keep flying the helicopter. You need to be in control of it, and set it up for the best possible result. Nothing is more important than flying the helicopter first.
N	Navigate	**Navigate** refers to, once the helicopter is under control, flying it somewhere safe. If possible maintain course or at least steer the helicopter to the most suitable landing area. It is one thing to be in control, it is another to be in control and make the helicopter go where you want it to go. You need to be doing both.
C	Communicate	**Communicate externally** by announcing what the emergency is on the radio.
		This means you will have to make a radio call to let others know of your problems, where you are and what you are going to do. Communicating is usually the last thing you do, not the first, but it is still very important so that you know that either help is on the way or, at the very least, others have been alerted to your problem. When communicating we want to follow a standard format so the calls are very predictable and able to be practised. The more you practice, the more automatic your response will be in a real situation, and the less mental energy you have to expend when all your focus should be on managing the helicopter and the emergency.
A	Administrate	Manage the emergency. This may include:
		- Activating emergency beacons and tracking equipment
		- Troubleshooting to try and fix the problem
		- Giving a passenger brief
		- Preparing for an emergency landing.
		It is very important to note here that these further checks are only considered if the crew has time. If they do not have time, ignore them and concentrate on flying the helicopter.

Priority

Whenever there is a MAYDAY or a PAN-PAN call given or heard, the aircraft making the transmission has priority.

This means that radio silence should be observed by all other aircraft unless they can offer assistance.

If other aircraft continue to transmit and are hindering distress of urgency communications, then ATC or another aircraft in control of the situation may make a broadcast telling everyone else to stay off the radio. The words used would be "***STOP TRANSMITTING: MAYDAY***".

This may have implications for those aircraft in a control zone that require clearances. In these situations, unless otherwise advised by ATC, continue with your last clearance and proceed with what would normally be expected of you even without a clearance.

> **Example**
>
> You are in the circuit downwind and have not yet been given a clearance to land. Another aircraft makes a MAYDAY call. The tower is concentrating on assisting them and is not able to give you a clearance to land. In this case, if it is safe to do so, land anyway and taxi to the parking area. Do not make any further radio calls, unless you deem it necessary and appropriate, or ATC advises that other aircraft can start communicating again.

Distress (MAYDAY)

Distress is defined as a condition of being **threatened by serious and/or imminent danger** and **requiring immediate assistance**. This can be the aircraft, the crew or passengers or something external that you can see.

The key word associated with a distress situation is ***MAYDAY.***

Examples of a distress situation could be:

- An engine failure
- A tail rotor drive shaft failure
- A fire in flight
- Severe vibrations and noises; and
- You see someone else in distress (a sinking boat) and assisting.

Making a MAYDAY Call

When the pilot of an aircraft is in distress, they must transmit on the radio frequency that will give them the best chance of being heard. Sometimes this is both.

For example, if operating OCTA low level on a local CTAF where no one else is listening, making a distress call on that frequency may not bring you assistance. Making the MAYDAY call on the local AREA frequency, where Centre and other aircraft are listening, has a much better chance of getting a response. This is the pilot's decision given the circumstances on the day.

Say the word MAYDAY three (3) times followed by the distress message.

The Distress message should have as many of the following list of items as the pilot deems necessary and appropriate.

- MAYDAY three (3) times
- Station called (e.g. Brisbane Centre, Sunshine Coast Tower, other aircraft)
- Helicopter callsign. If possible three (3) times
- Current position, height and intentions
- Nature of the distress situation
- POB (People On Board)

It is important to note here that helicopter pilots typically say less because they operate very close to the ground and do not have time to transmit much information, also they typically remain within 1-5NM of the original distress call where as a fixed-wing at very high altitudes may travel 100s of miles from where the original MAYDAY call was made.

Example of a MAYDAY call

Example of a MAYDAY call in the event of an engine failure.

	Action	Discussion
1	Communicate	Announce the emergency
2	Aviate	Enter autorotation
3	Navigate	Turn into wind and pick a landing site
4	Communicate	*"MAYDAY MAYDAY MAYDAY* *Brisbane Centre this is* *WCF, WCF, WCF* *10NM West of the Sunshine Coast at 1500 feet with an engine failure conducting an autorotation into the bottom of a valley POB 2"*
5	Administrate	Manage the emergency. (See *After a MAYDAY or PAN -PAN Radio Call*)

Urgency (PAN-PAN)

Urgency is defined as a condition concerning the safety of an aircraft, or some person on board or within sight, but which **does not require immediate assistance**.

The key word associated with an urgency situation is ***PAN-PAN.***

Examples of an urgency situation could be:

- A hydraulic failure that the pilot is not comfortable with
- A warning or caution light
- Low fuel situation
- Deteriorating weather where the pilot is in a compromised position; or
- Someone on the ground needing assistance.

Making a PAN-PAN Call

When the pilot of an aircraft is in an urgent situation, they must transmit on the radio frequency that will give them the best chance of being heard.

For example, if operating OCTA low level on a local CTAF where no one else is listening, making an urgency call on that frequency may not bring you assistance. Making the same radio call on the local AREA frequency where Centre and other aircraft are listening, has a much better chance of getting a response. This is at the pilot's decision given the circumstances on the day.

Say the word PAN-PAN three (3) times followed by the urgent message.

The Urgent message should have as many of the following list of items as the pilot deems necessary and appropriate.

- PAN-PAN three (3) times
- Station called (e.g. Brisbane Centre, Sunshine Coast Tower, other aircraft)
- Helicopter callsign. If possible three (3) times
- Current position, height and intentions
- Nature of the urgent situation

It is important to note here that the pilot may be able to give more detailed information in a PAN-PAN call as the helicopter is not "crashing" but still flying but the pilot has some concern over something that needs to be communicated.

Example of a PAN-PAN call

Example of a PAN-PAN call in the event of a hydraulic failure:

	Action	Discussion
1	Communicate	Announce the emergency
2	Aviate	Establish the helicopter in straight and level flight at 60-70 knots.
3	Navigate	Run through the emergency checklist actions, then come up with a plan (CANCA). If the crew thinks it is warranted given the circumstances, then continue with the Urgency call. This will give the helicopter priority with ATC and will alert them to your situation. There will be situations where the crew does not think it is warranted to make a PAN-PAN call after a hydraulic failure. It is completely up to the crew to make the decision based on their circumstances.
4	Communicate	*"PAN-PAN, PAN-PAN, PAN-PAN* *Sunshine Coast Tower this is* *WCF, WCF, WCF* *10NM West of the Sunshine Coast at 1500 feet with a hydraulic failure. We would like to join straight in for a landing on Runway 12"*
5	Administrate	Manage the situation. (See *After a MAYDAY or PAN-PAN Radio Call*)

Emergency change of level

When operating within controlled airspace and there is a requirement to make a rapid change in altitude because of:

- Technical problems (engine failure, de-pressurisation, fire etc.)
- Severe weather conditions (hail, icing, turbulence)
- Some other reason

Then conduct the following:

	Action	Discussion
1	Communicate	Announce the situation.
2	Aviate	Establish control of the helicopter.
3	Navigate	Establish the helicopter in an emergency descent in a safe direction. Squawk 7700 on the transponder.
4	Communicate	*"PAN-PAN, PAN-PAN, PAN-PAN* *Brisbane Approach this is* *WCF, WCF, WCF* *10NM West of Brisbane at 8500 feet conducting an emergency descent due to an engine fire. We would like to join straight in for a landing on Runway 14 or will terminate prior to the airport if possible"*
5	Administrate	Manage the situation (See *After a MAYDAY or PAN-PAN Radio Call*).

After a MAYDAY or PAN-PAN Radio Call

Following on from the radio call the following actions will help ATC and Search and Rescue assist you quickly.

- ELT ON (AMSA via satellite)
- Transponder squawk 7700 for emergency (ATC identification on radar)
- Switch any additional tracking equipment installed to EMERGENCY.

If the crew has time, they may wish to manage the situation by:

- **Troubleshooting** to try to fix the problem
- **Preparing** for an emergency landing by shutting down the fuel and ignition, if appropriate.
- Give a **passenger brief**. This should be short and only a confirmation of the pre-flight passenger brief already given. For example BRACE, BRACE, BRACE.

It is very important to note here that these further checks are only considered if the crew has time. If they do not have time, ignore them and concentrate on flying the helicopter.

After landing

After landing from a Distress or Urgency situation or if the situation changes, then there will be three (3) possible outcomes.

- The Distress or Urgent situation resolves itself and no longer exists. In this case contact ATC and cancel the MAYDAY or PAN -PAN call and resume *"Operations Normal"*.
- The crew are fit and healthy and able to conduct some post-landing actions; or
- The crew is incapacitated and will need assistance, in which case they are not likely to be able to do any post-landing actions.

Post landing actions

If the crew is fit and healthy, then when on the ground:

- The priority is the safety of any passengers and crew who shall be evacuated.
- Secure the aircraft.
- Make sure the ELT is activated (ON) or deactivated (OFF) depending on the circumstances.
- If the landing is
    - outside an airport where there is no ATC, then make contact with the Company and/or ATC to let them know the outcome.
    - at an airport with ATC, then the outcome should be known so in the first instance make contact with the Company.

Activation of the ELT

The Emergency Locator Transmitter (ELT) is an electronic radio device that has its own internal batteries that can be either activated manually by the pilot or automatically activated when in the ARM position in the event of a hard landing.

Activating the ELT

If the pilot needs to activate the ELT:

1. Press the **red toggle button** to the **ON position**, and
2. Hold it in for at least **1 second to activate**.

It will transmit on two (2) frequencies:

- VHF 121.5 MHz. This is an analogue signal that can be received by the aircraft's VHF radio and will transmit the moment the unit is switched on; and
- 406MHz (and sometimes 243MHz). This is a digital signal which automatically sends a message to a satellite and then communicates with the relevant Search and Rescue authority in the nearest Country. This can take up to 50 seconds for the signal from the ELT to get to the satellite so the sooner it is turned on the better.

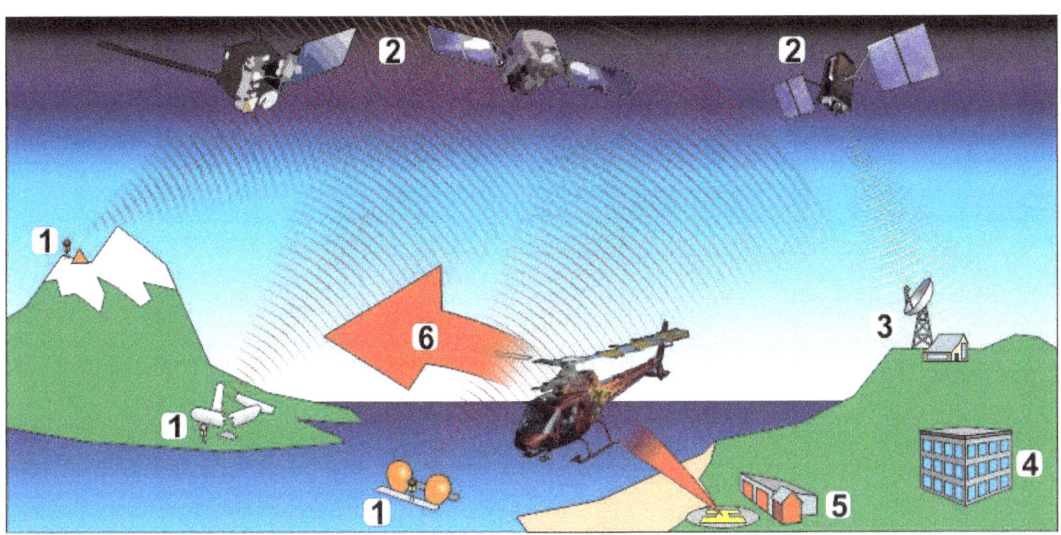

1 = Triggered emergency beacon
2 = Search and Rescue satellites
3 = Local user terminal
4 = Mission control centre
5 = Rescue coordination centre

On leaving the satellite, it may also have to go through a local user terminal and a mission control centre, before coming to the local Rescue Co-ordination Centre depending on where the distressed ship or aircraft is.

In Australia, the signal arrives at the Australian Maritime Safety Authority (AMSA) which have a Rescue Co-ordination Centre (RCC) in Canberra to coordinate any search and rescues activated by receiving a signal from an ELT.

Types of ELT

There are two (2) main types of ELT in aircraft.

Aircraft installed ELT: This is a unit that is bolted into the aircraft and is integrated into the aircraft's systems. It will have an external aerial, and a switching unit that the pilot can operate from the cockpit. It has its own internal batteries that must be replaced every 12 or 24 months so it will work independently of the aircraft's electrical system.

Portable or Personal ELT referred to as a PLB: This is a smaller unit that a pilot can purchase and hold as a personal ELT carried on the pilot. It does not activate automatically and must be turned ON by the pilot. It also has batteries that must be replaced every 12-24 months but it also must be checked monthly to confirm its status.

Maritime (ships) also have a locator beacon but it is referred to as an Emergency Position Indicating Radio Beacon (EPIRB). It operates in the same manner as an ELT but is usually designed to be waterproof and float.

Testing and Inadvertent Activation

If the ELT is inadvertently activated for periods longer than 10 seconds, then the crew is required:

- during flight, contact ATC and tell them the ELT was inadvertently activated.
- when on the ground, phone RCC on 1800815257 and tell them it was inadvertently activated.

ELTs often require testing. This should only be done in the first five (5) minutes of each hour and for no more than three (3) audio sweeps of the signal. Before testing, tune the VHF radio to 121.5 and listen out on that frequency. Within the first 5 minutes past the hour, activate the ELT and listen for the loud distress signal. Turn it OFF before the three (3) audio pulses.

Aviation Communication and Flight Radio *for Helicopter Pilots*

Examples of Radio Calls

Aim

This chapter aims to:

- Give examples of typical radio calls that a trainee can use.

Related documents

- Flight Radio for Helicopter Pilots
- ERSA
- AIP
- AIP GEN 3.4

Introduction to Making Radio Calls

Although radio calls are reasonably predictable, it still takes time and practice for pilots to be comfortable in making them. In this chapter, we have scripted some common radio calls that can be used as examples and help pilots in creating their own radio calls based on their unique circumstances.

Although calls can take a standard format, there may be some differences based on local knowledge, the category of operation and the type of operation.

Local Knowledge is specific to an aerodrome and is knowledge gained by a pilot or an operator having been to that aerodrome before or being based at the aerodrome.

The category of operation will be divided into:

- VFR
- NVFR
- IFR; and
- NVG.

The type of operation can vary considerably, below are some examples:

- Flight training
- Agriculture
- Fire fighting
- Sling
- Photography; and
- SAR/EMS, etc.

What this means is there may be additional information that has to be put in the radio call that is not typically standard. This information is designed to help ATC give you the clearance you want and need. Without this information you may be given clearances you do not want and cannot abide by.

Just what extra information you need to put in will come with experience.

Local Knowledge

Local knowledge may have the local ATC asking or wanting some specific information. If this is the airport that you usually operate from, then to help ATC you may give this information before they ask because you have local knowledge.

Unlike Class C aerodromes, Class D aerodromes do not require a flight plan to be lodged before the flight, so the controller will have no prior knowledge of your flight. For this reason, the Ground Controller likes pilots to establish communication and have the pilot state in that initial call if they are staying in the local area or departing the control zone before providing full details.

This allows the ATC controller to obtain the correct coloured information strip which they will write on and then place on their control board.

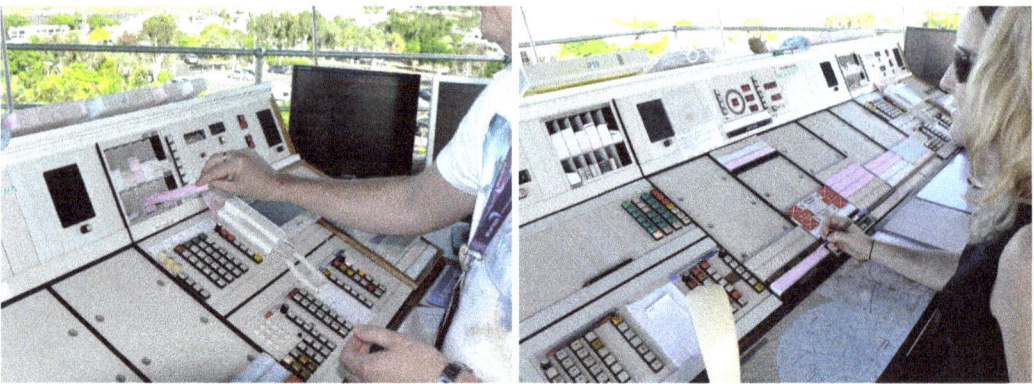

Without this information, they will have to wait for you to make the full radio call before they know which colour strip they have to write on. This means they have to try to remember what you have said and then there will be a delay in their response as they are writing it down.

The controllers have four (4) different coloured strips to write on as follows:

Colour	Meaning
Yellow	A Yellow strip is created for any VFR or IFR aircraft that is **INBOUND** to the aerodrome.
Blue	A Blue strip is created for any VFR or IFR aircraft that is **OUTBOUND** from the aerodrome.
Pink	A Pink strip is created for any miscellaneous items that may come up that does not fit into a specific category.
	Any local aircraft that is leaving the control zone, but coming back (referred to as local return flights).
	Any IFR aerial work or training flights that enter the control zone, but do not land.
	Any photography, sling, agriculture or survey work are all examples of a Pink strip.
White	A White strip is created for any circuit or HTA operations.

> **Example**
>
> Consider a helicopter about to call Ground for operations in the local training area, the Establish Comms radio call may be as follows:
>
> *"Sunshine Coast Ground Helicopter WCF for the Helicopter Training Area"*
>
> The controller now knows that you are staying local, will then obtain the White coloured strip and reply:
>
> *"WCF, Sunshine Coast Ground, go ahead"*
>
> You can now continue with the full radio call.
>
> *"WCF Bell 206 on the western apron, Received Alpha, POB 2 Dual, request taxi to pad Juliet"*

Category of operation

When calling ATC, unless it is DAY VFR, they want to know the category. This means when on an IFR flight plan, tell them "IFR" in the radio call. When NVFR or NVG, tell them NVFR or NVG in the radio call.

> **Example**
>
> Consider an IFR training flight departing for Kingaroy at 6000, the radio call may be as follows:
>
> *"Sunshine Coast Ground, Helicopter WCF Bell 206, on the western apron, IFR, received Alpha, POB 2 Dual, for Kingaroy request taxi and airways clearance"*

Type of operation

Helicopters typically operate differently from fixed-wing aircraft. Fixed-wing operations are usually very predictable and standard, so standard radio calls will work.

In the helicopter world, because of the tasks helicopters are expected to complete, we are often doing things that are not standard and, therefore, telling ATC on the radio of anything specific to the operation will help them manage the flight better, as well as manage other aircraft around our specific operation.

> **Examples**
>
> ### Training Flights
>
> If departing on a training flight, if ATC knows the trainee is solo or that there is an instructor on board, this may change the type of clearance they give you and may also change how they speak to you. Typically students going solo are given easier airways clearances and the tower will not expect you to know everything. They will look after you. If an instructor is on board then ATC will expect that the instructor knows what to do and they will "trust" the aircraft more.
>
> *For example:*
>
> Consider a training flight into the helicopter training area with an instructor and two students on board at a Class D aerodrome. The relevant information the controller would like to know is how many people are on board and if it is a training flight is it dual or solo? The radio call may be as follows:
>
> *"Sunshine Coast Ground, Helicopter WCF Bell 206 on the western apron, Received Alpha POB 3 Dual request taxi to pad Delta"*

Examples

Agricultural flying

If agricultural flying with a load of heavy chemicals, you may not be able to do a normal taxi or take-off so telling ATC this in the call will again help them manage you better.

For example:

Consider an agricultural flight where the helicopter is departing for low-level spraying operations inside the control zone. The radio call may be as follows

"Sunshine Coast Ground, Helicopter WCF Bell 206, at the Beckers Hanger, received Alpha for low-level agricultural ops 2NM to the east of the field below 300 request departure from our current position"

SAR or EMS

If on a SAR or EMS flight, ATC may give you a different priority and a clearance that gets you to your destination faster.

For example:

Consider an EMS flight departing IFR for Kingaroy at 5000. The radio call may be as follows

"Sunshine Coast Ground, Helicopter WCF Bell 206, at the Careflight Hanger, IFR, received Alpha, MED 1 for Kingaroy at 5000 request airways clearance"

Photography

If conducting a photography flight, telling ATC what you want to do allows them to plan for it. The variations in the radio calls are many so the content may have to be changed to take this into account.

For example:

Consider a photography job inside the control zone where you need to operate between 500 and 1500 feet in a particular area. The radio call may be as follows

"Sunshine Coast Ground, Helicopter WCF Bell 206, at Beckers South, received Alpha for aerial photography over Twin Waters Resort not above 1500 feet request taxi to pad Delta"

Class D No radar CTR Calls – Procedural Aerodrome

When entering a Class D aerodrome Control Zone (CTR) below the Control Area (CTA) step, then an *"Implied Airways Clearance"* is acceptable.

Example Radio Calls

In the following topics, there are examples of radio calls made by VFR helicopters at a CTR. They are the minimum calls required. Additional radio calls may have to be made based on the requirements of the Tower controller at the time.

The calls are made in the following format:

- calls by the pilot are in *blue* with a callsign of WCF; and
- ATC calls are in *green*.

Outbound: Class D no radar CTR Calls – procedural aerodrome

ATIS	Listen to and note the ATIS.
Ground	*Sunshine Coast Ground, Helicopter WCF for Gympie*
	WCF, Sunshine Coast Ground
	WCF, Bell 206, Western Apron, POB 2, Dual, received Alpha, request taxi to pad Juliet
	WCF time 25 taxi pad Juliet call tower when ready
	Taxi Pad Juliet WCF
Tower	*Sunshine Coast Tower, WCF for Gympie 1500 Pad Juliet Ready*
	WCF, Sunshine Coast Tower, Pad Juliet cleared for take-off make left turn
	Cleared for take-off make left turn WCF

Inbound: Class D no radar CTR Calls – procedural aerodrome

ATIS	Listen to and note the ATIS.
Tower	*Sunshine Coast Tower, Helicopter WCF with inbound details*
	WCF, Sunshine Coast Tower
	WCF, Bell 206, received Alpha, 10NM to the South at 1500 inbound for Pad Juliet
	WCF, track direct, report right base
	WCF
	— — —
	WCF right base Pad Juliet
	WCF cleared to land
	Cleared to land, WCF
Ground	*Sunshine Coast Ground, WCF, Pad Juliet, request taxi to the western apron*
	WCF, Sunshine Coast Ground, taxi for the western apron
	WCF

Operating in the Control Zone: Class D no radar CTR Calls – procedural aerodrome

ATIS	Listen to and note the ATIS.
Ground	*Sunshine Coast Ground, Helicopter WCF for the Helicopter Training Area*
	WCF, Sunshine Coast Ground
	WCF, Bell 206, Western apron, received information Alpha, POB 2 Dual request taxi to pad Juliet
	WCF time 25 taxi pad Juliet call tower when ready
	Taxi Pad Juliet WCF
Tower	*Sunshine Coast Tower, WCF for operations in the Helicopter Training Area not above 500 Pad Juliet Ready*
	WCF, Sunshine Coast Tower, Pad Juliet cleared for take-off call established in the Helicopter Training Area
	Cleared for take-off wilco WCF

— — —

WCF established in the helicopter Training Area, will call operations normal by time 30

WCF

— — —

WCF Operations normal, again on the hour

WCF

— — —

WCF operations Complete in the Helicopter Training Area, request transit to the western apron

WCF transit to the western apron

WCF

Ground	*Sunshine Coast Ground, WCF*
	WCF, Sunshine Coast Ground

Aviation Communication and Flight Radio *for Helicopter Pilots*

Class D no radar CTA Calls – procedural airspace

When entering a Class D aerodrome Control Area (CTA) above the Control Zone (CTR) step, then a full airways clearance is required.

The following are examples of radio calls made by VFR helicopters at a CTA. They are the minimum calls required. Additional radio calls may have to be made based on the requirements of the Tower controller at the time.

The calls are made in the following format:

- calls by the pilot are in *blue* with a callsign of WCF; and
- ATC calls are in *green*.

Outbound: Class D no radar CTA Calls – procedural airspace

ATIS	*Listen to and note the ATIS.*
Ground	Sunshine Coast Ground, Helicopter WCF for Gympie.
	WCF, Sunshine Coast Ground
	WCF, Bell 206, Western Apron, received information Alpha, POB 2 Dual for Gympie direct at 2500 request taxi to pad Juliet and airways clearance.
	WCF time 25. Clearance track direct to Gympie at 2500, taxi pad Juliet time 25
	Track direct to Gympie at 2500, taxi Pad Juliet, WCF.
Tower	Sunshine Coast Tower, WCF Pad Juliet, Ready.
	WCF, Sunshine Coast Tower, Pad Juliet cleared for take-off make left turn.
	Cleared for take-off make left turn WCF.

— — —

WCF departed 15 tracking 302 for Gympie on climb to 2500

WCF report when clear of the zone

WCF

— — —

WCF clear of the zone

WCF frequency change approved

WCF

Mike Becker, Becker Helicopters

Inbound: Class D no radar CTA Calls – procedural airspace

ATIS — Listen to and note the ATIS.

Tower — Sunshine Coast Tower, Helicopter WCF with inbound details

> WCF, Sunshine Coast Tower

ND, Bell 206, received Alpha, 10NM to the south of the field at 2500 inbound for a landing at Pad Juliet request airways clearance

> WCF, track direct to the field, maintain 2500 report when crossing the Maroochy River bridge

Track direct to the field at 2500 and call crossing the Maroochy River Bridge, WCF

— — —

WCF crossing the Maroochy River Bridge

> WCF cleared visual approach, report right base Pad Juliet

Cleared visual approach report right base Pad Juliet, WCF

— — —

WCF, right base Pad Juliet

> WCF cleared to land contact ground 121.1

Cleared to land, contact ground 121.1, WCF

Ground — Sunshine Coast Ground, WCF Pad Juliet request taxi to the western apron

> WCF, Sunshine Coast Ground cleared to taxi to the western apron

Taxi to the western apron WCF

> WCF report on the ground

Report on the ground WCF

— — —

WCF on the ground

> WCF

Class D CTA Calls for IFR flights

When entering a Class D aerodrome Control Area (CTA) above the Control Zone (CTR) step then a full airways clearance is required.

The following are examples of radio calls made by VFR helicopters at a CTA. They are the minimum calls required. Additional radio calls may have to be made based on the requirements of the Tower controller at the time.

The calls are made in the following format:

- calls by the pilot are in *blue* with a callsign of WCF; and
- ATC calls are in *green*.

Outbound: Class D CTA Calls for IFR flights

ATIS	*Listen to and note the ATIS.*
Ground	*Sunshine Coast Ground, Helicopter WCF Bell 206, western apron IFR, POB 2 Dual, received Alpha for Kingaroy 6000 request taxi and airways clearance*
	WCF, Sunshine Coast Ground, Cleared to track direct to Kingaroy 6000 squawk 4132, taxi pad Juliet, time 25
	Cleared direct to Kingaroy 6000, squawk 4132, taxi Pad Juliet WCF
Tower	*Sunshine Coast Tower, Helicopter WCF, Pad Juliet for an overhead departure, ready*
	WCF, Sunshine Coast Tower cleared for takeoff make right turn
	Cleared for takeoff make right turn WCF
	— — —
	WCF tracking the 270 radial reference the Sunshine Coast VOR on climb to 6000
	WCF report passing 3000
	WCF
	— — —
	WCF passing 3000
	WCF contact Brisbane Centre on 129.0
	129.0 WCF
FIA	*Brisbane Centre Helicopter 8 GPM on the 270 radial climbing to 6000*
	WCF identified, no known IFR traffic
	WCF

Inbound: Class D CTA Calls for IFR flights

ATIS	Listen to and note the ATIS.
FIA	*WCF Brisbane Centre at 25NM Sunshine Coast contact Sunshine Coast Tower on 124.4*
	At 25NM contact Sunshine Coast Tower on 124.4 WCF
Tower	*Sunshine Coast Tower, Helicopter WCF, IFR, received Alpha, in cloud, 25GPS on the 270 radial reference the VOR on descent from 6000 inbound for a VOR Alpha approach and sector entry request airways clearance*
	WCF, Sunshine Coast Tower continue descent to 2800, track direct to the field expect the VOR Alpha approach, report overhead the aid
	Track direct to the field, continue descent to 2800 and call over the aid WCF
	— — —
	WCF overhead the aid ready for a sector entry and VOR Alpha approach
	WCF make the sector entry and report when overhead ready for the approach maintain 2800 feet
	Make sector entry, call overhead the aid when ready for the outbound leg and maintain 2800 WCF
	— — —
	WCF overhead the aid ready for the approach
	WCF cleared the VOR Alpha approach report again at the final approach fix
	Cleared the VOR Alpha approach WCF
	— — —
	WCF final approach fix
	WCF roger what are your intentions at the minima
	WCF when visual we would like to circle for a landing on Pad Delta
	WCF Pad Delta cleared to land
	Cleared to land, WCF
Ground	*Sunshine Coast Ground WCF, Pad Delta request taxi to the western apron*
	WCF Sunshine Coast Ground cleared to taxi to the western apron via taxiway Delta and Echo
	Taxi to the western apron via Delta and Echo WCF

Aviation Communication and Flight Radio *for Helicopter Pilots*

Class C Radar Control Zones with separate ACD and Ground

Inbound: Class C Radar Control Zones with separate ACD and Ground

ATIS	Listen to and note the ATIS.	
FIA	Brisbane Centre Helicopter WCF Bell 206 overhead Roys Orchard 1500 inbound for the Brisbane GA request code	
	WCF, Brisbane Centre remain outside controlled airspace squawk 1234	
	Remain outside controlled airspace squawk 1234 WCF	
	WCF Brisbane Centre identified, confirm altitude	
	WCF 1500	
	WCF roger contact Brisbane Approach 124.6 approaching Beachmere	
	Contact Brisbane Approach 124.6 at Beachmere WCF	
Brisbane Approach	Brisbane Approach WCF request clearance received Alpha	
	WCF Brisbane Approach track via the Hornibrook viaduct for the Brisbane GA, QNH 1021 Maintain 1500	
	Track via the Hornibrook viaduct for the Brisbane GA, 1500, QNH 1021 WCF	
	— — —	
	WCF contact Brisbane Tower 120.5	
	Contact Brisbane Tower 120.5 WCF	
Tower	Brisbane Tower WCF Hornibrook viaduct 1500 for the Brisbane GA	
	WCF Brisbane Tower track direct to the Brisbane GA, make visual approach to the Helipad on Foxtrot 4 remain west of runway 19/01	
	Track direct, make visual approach to Helipad on Foxtrot 4 remain west of runway 19/01 WCF	
	— — —	
	WCF finals for helipad on Foxtrot 4	
	WCF call ground 121.9 for traffic on the GA area	
	Contact Ground 121.9 WCF	
Ground	Brisbane Ground WCF finals for the Helipad on Foxtrot 4	
	WCF, Brisbane Ground, no known traffic on the GA Area cleared to land	
	— — —	
	WCF request taxi to parking	
	WCF taxi to parking	
	WCF	

Outbound: Class C Radar Control Zones with separate ACD and Ground

ATIS	Listen to and note the ATIS.
ACD	*Brisbane Delivery Helicopter WCF for the Sunshine Coast request clearance*
	WCF Brisbane Delivery track Sunshine Coast via the Hornibrook viaduct at 1500, squawk 1245, contact ground 121.9 for taxi
	Clearance track Sunshine Coast via the Hornibrook viaduct at 1500 squawk 1245, contact Ground 121.9 for taxi, WCF
Ground	*Brisbane Ground Helicopter WCF Bell 206, POB 2, received Alpha, Brisbane GA request taxi to the Helipad*
	WCF, Brisbane Ground, taxi to and hold short of the Helipad on Foxtrot 4, call Tower 120.5 when ready
	Taxi to and hold short helipad on Foxtrot 4, contact Tower 120.5 when ready, WCF
Tower	*Brisbane Tower, Helicopter WCF Helipad on Foxtrot 4, ready*
	WCF Brisbane Tower, remaining west of 01/19 cleared for take-off make early left turn, call when airborne
	Cleared for take-off make left turn, remaining west of 01/19 call when airborne, WCF
	— — —
	WCF airborne
	WCF roger contact Brisbane Departures 128.3
	Contact Departures 128.3 , WCF
Brisbane Departures	*Brisbane Departures, WCF passing through 800 on climb to 1500*
	WCF identified
	WCF
	— — —
	WCF leaving radar controlled area radar services are terminated, contact Brisbane Centre on 125.7
	Contact Brisbane Centre 125.7 WCF
FIA	*Brisbane Centre, Helicopter WCF maintaining 1500*
	WCF Brisbane Centre

Class G Non-towered aerodrome – CTAF procedures

Inbound: Class G Non-towered aerodrome – CTAF procedures

ATIS or AWIS Listen to and note the ATIS, AWIS, AWIB or WATIR if available.

CTAF frequency

All stations Gympie, Helicopter WCF Bell 206 12NM to the west at 2500 feet inbound, estimate the circuit at 37 Gympie

— — —

Gympie Traffic, Helicopter WCF is the circuit area joining left base for runway 32 for a landing at the southern helipad Gympie

— — —

Gympie Traffic Helicopter WCF taxing to parking, clear of the runway

Outbound: Class G Non-towered aerodrome – CTAF procedures

ATIS or AWIS Listen to and note the ATIS, AWIS, AWIB or WATIR if available

CTAF frequency

Gympie Traffic Helicopter WCF Bell 206 at the apron taxing to the southern helipad

— — —

Gympie Traffic, Helicopter WCF Bell 206 rolling parallel to runway 32 with a right turn for the Sunshine Coast, Gympie

— — —

All stations Gympie, Helicopter WCF departed the circuit this time tracking 150 on climb to 2500 for the Sunshine Coast, Gympie

Radio Waves and Frequencies

Aim

This chapter aims to:

- Explain radio waves and frequencies
- List the frequency bands
- Explain what factors affect radio waves.

Level of Competency

On successful completion of this lesson, the trainee will be able to:

- Draw a radio wave and label its components
- State the aviation frequency band names.

Radio Waves

To understand radio waves we need to understand energy and how it is transferred or transported in the world around us.

Mechanical waves

Think of a rock being dropped into a pond of water. Where the rock hits the water, it will transfer energy and an observer will see a ripple or a "shock wave" expand outwards from where the rock entered the water.

The bigger the rock the bigger the energy wave or the harder the rock was thrown at the water the bigger the energy wave. This example shows the properties of waves and how they move. It shows a wavelength, frequency and amplitude.

It is very important to note that the water does not travel away from the rock, but it is the energy that is transferred from one water particle to another that allows the energy wave to move outwards and we see this as the ever-expanding ripple on the water.

The further the wave gets from the source the bigger its coverage, but the weaker or smaller the wave. This is because the energy decreases the further it travels until it dies out completely.

Whatever these energy waves have to travel through (liquid, gas, solid or plasma) is called a medium. The thicker or denser the medium, the less the distance travelled, but the faster the wave can move.

This principle works very well when there is a medium for the energy to travel through, but what about in the vacuum of space? If there is no medium, then the energy wave cannot be transmitted from one particle to another particle because there aren't any! This is why there is no sound in space (a vacuum).

Sound waves on earth

No sound waves in space

Electromagnetic waves

Electricity and magnetism can together create their own electromagnetic waves in a similar manner to the waves described previously, but they do not need a medium to move and can travel at the speed of light. Radio waves are electromagnetic waves generated by electricity and magnetism that are produced within the electrical circuitry of the radio transmitter/receiver (transceiver). This electromagnetic wave can travel outwards from the source at the speed of light and, in theory, will keep travelling to infinity or until the signal gets so weak it simply dies out.

The electromagnetic wave will also have a wavelength, frequency and amplitude.

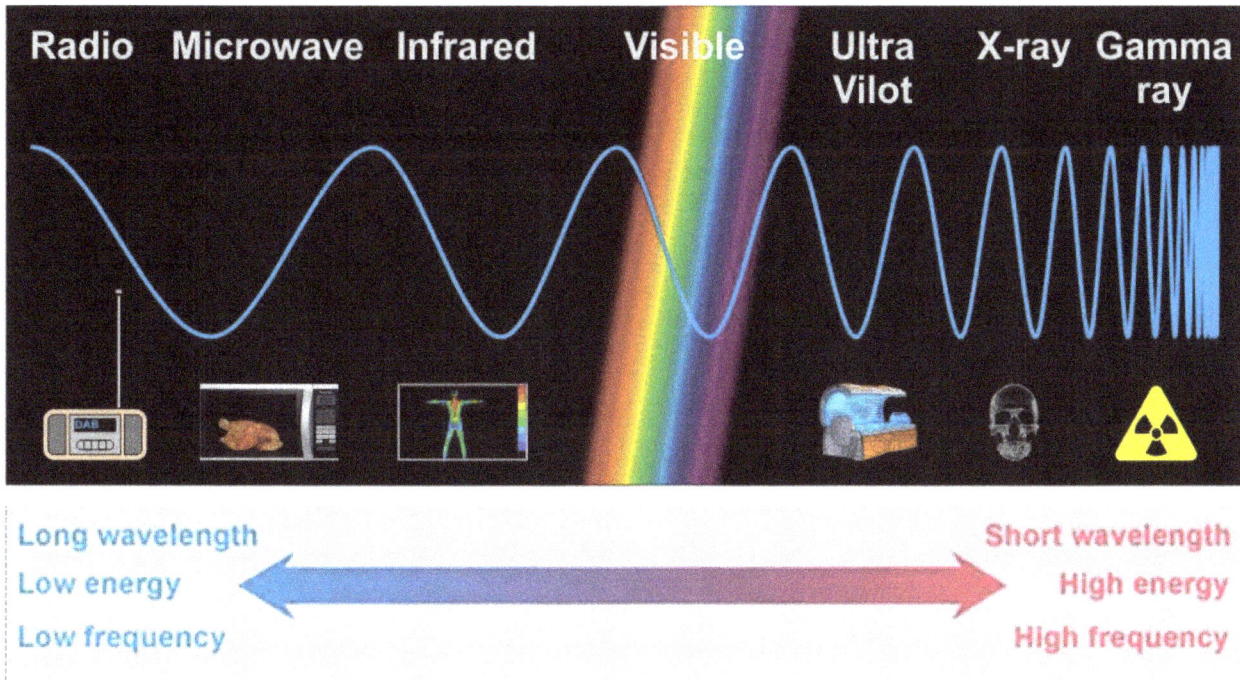

Describing electromagnetic energy

When an energy wave moves, it does so at a particular wavelength, at a particular frequency, at a given amplitude.

If you go back to the rock in the water example, the wavelength can be described as the distance between the same two points on each wave.

In the example below, we have used the wave crests as the same two points.

The amplitude can be described as how high each wave is relative to a median line, and the frequency can be described as the number of waves passing a particular point every second.

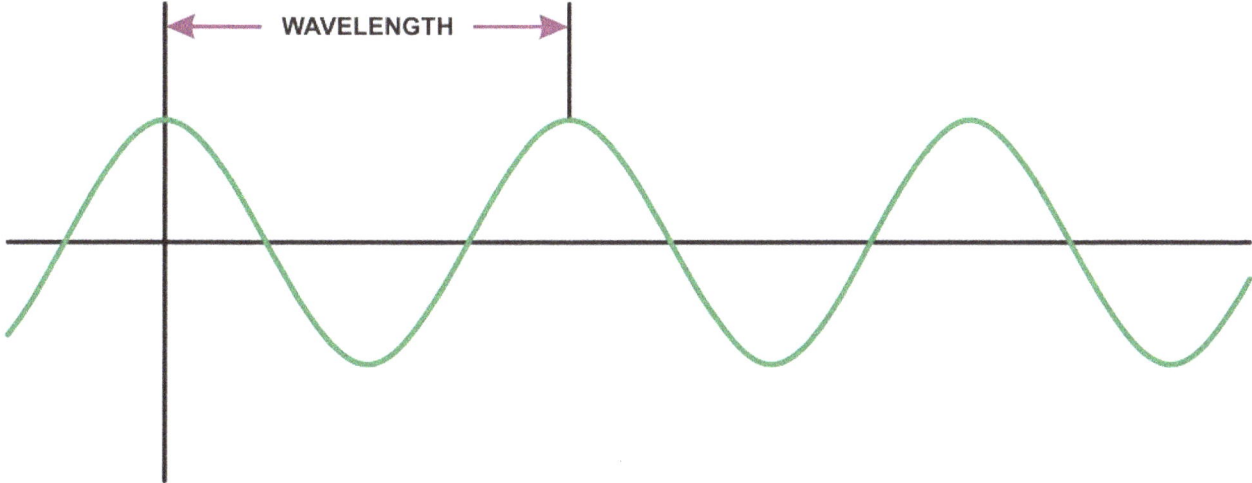

Amplitude

The amplitude of a wave describes its energy. Just like any wave, the bigger it is, the more energy it holds.

Picture an ocean wave. Two separate sets of waves can be coming in at the same frequency and have the same distance between each wave, but the bigger the wave, the more energy it holds. This represents amplitude.

Small wave   **Large wave**

The amplitude is measured from the base of the wave to the top of the wave in both a positive (up) and negative (down) relative to the median line.

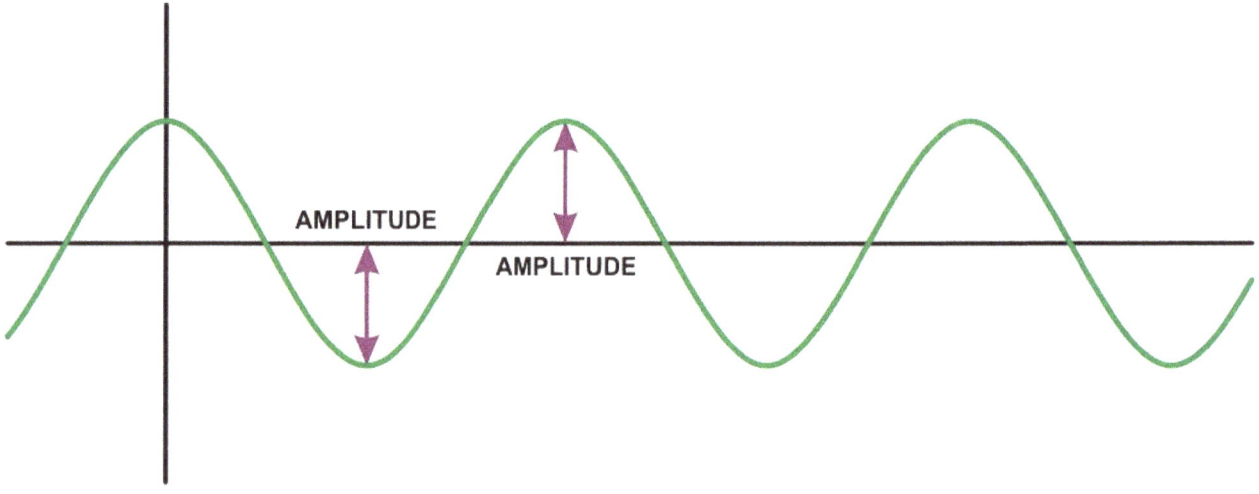

Wavelength and frequency

The wavelength of the electromagnetic wave is inversely proportional to the frequency of the wave. That is, the lower the frequency (the fewer number of waves passing a particular point) the longer the wavelength.

The key point to remember is the higher the frequency (the higher number of waves passing a particular point), the shorter the wavelength.

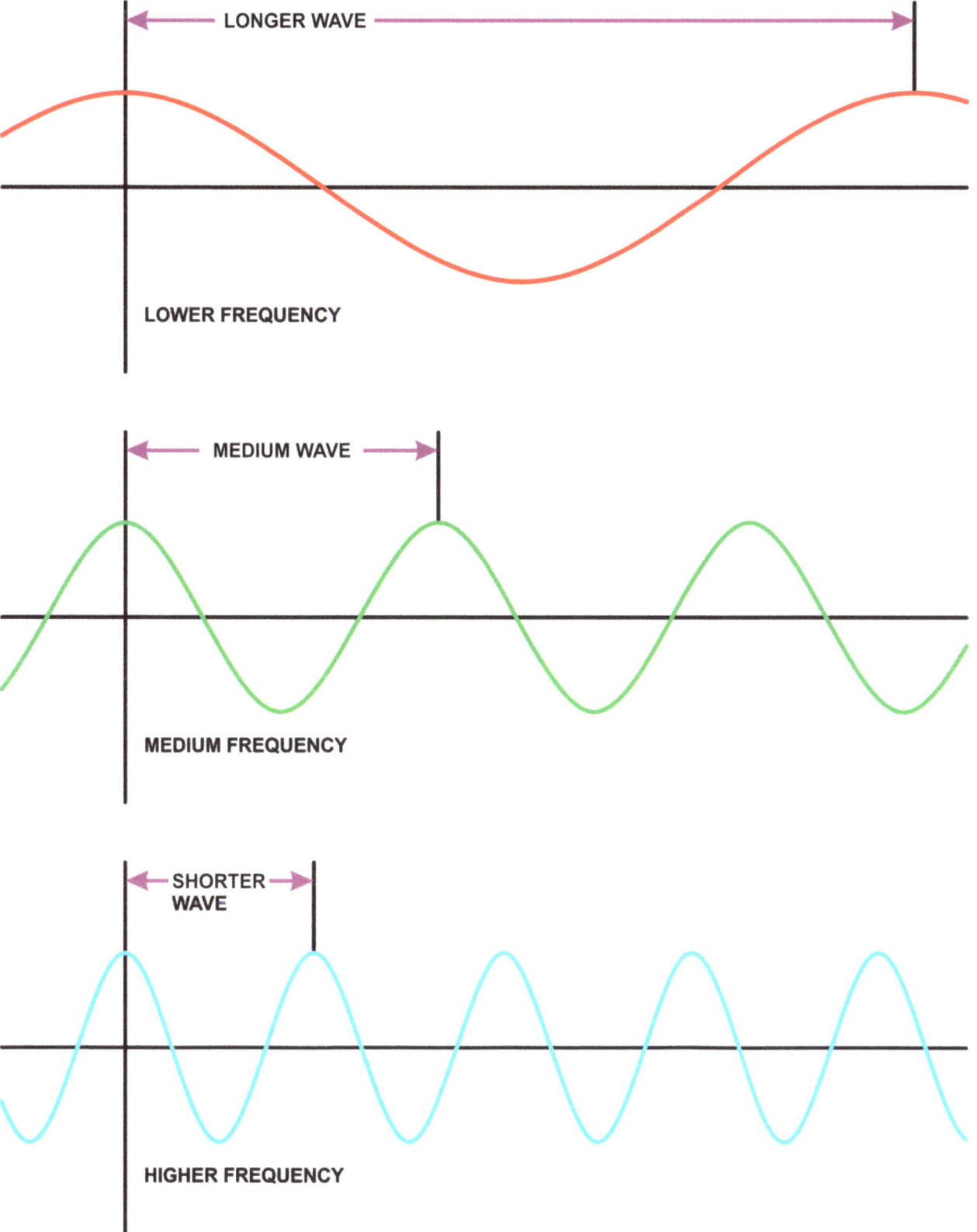

Hertz (Hz)

The frequency of the wave is measured in the number of times the same point of each new wave passes the same reference point and is counted in cycles per second (cps). In technical terms, this is called a **hertz (Hz),** after the German physicist discovered that waves have an oscillating frequency.

- One wave per second past a given point is given a frequency of 1Hz.
- Two waves per second past a given point is given a frequency of 2Hz.
- 1000 waves per second past a given point is given a frequency of 1000Hz or 1kHz (kilohertz where kilo means 1000).
- 1,000,000 waves per second past a given point is given a frequency of 1,000,000Hz, 1000kHz or 1 MHz (megahertz where mega means 1 million).
- 1,000,000,000,000 waves per second past a given point is given a frequency of 1,000,000,000,000Hz, 1,000,000MHz or 1GHz (Gigahertz where giga means 1 billion).

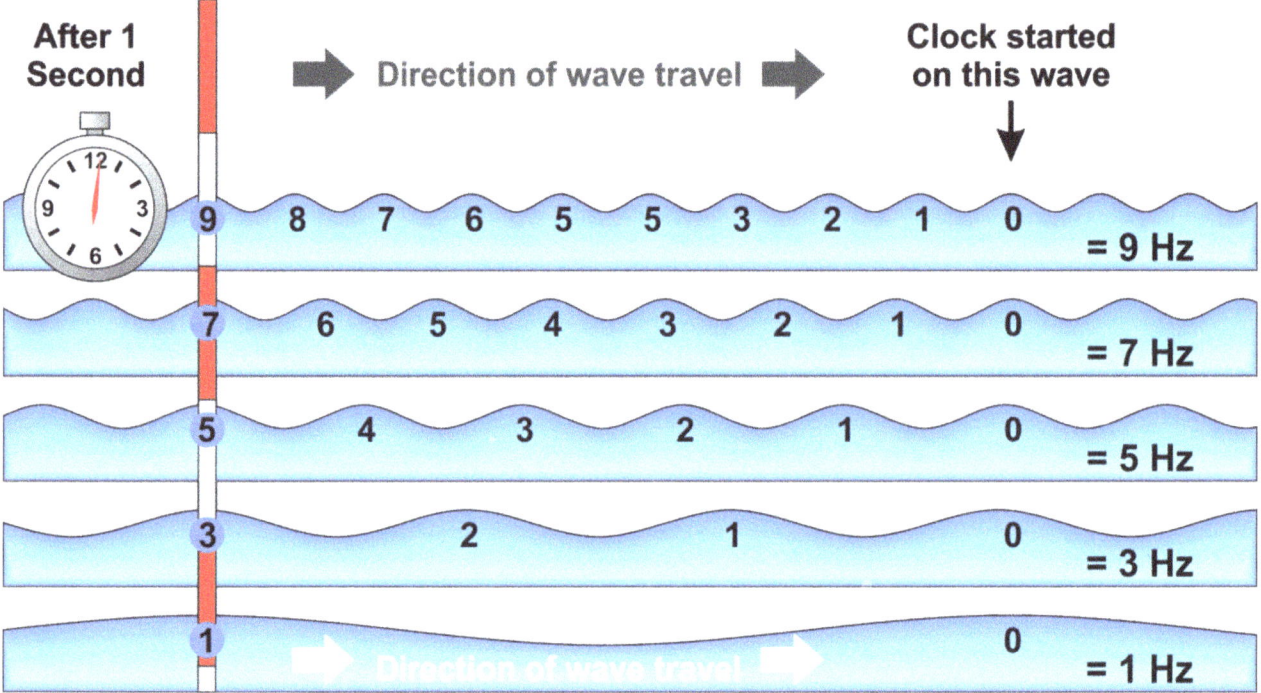

Audio Frequencies

The human ear can hear frequencies ranging between approximately 20Hz and 20,000Hz (20kHz).

Frequencies in the 20Hz to 20kHz range are referred to as the *Audio or Audible Frequencies* because they are the frequencies we as humans can hear.

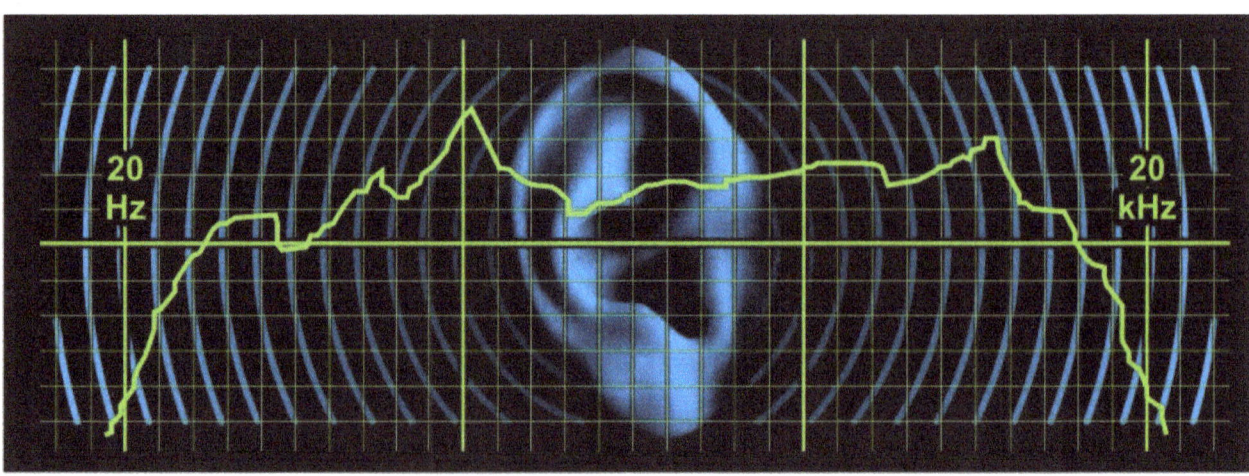

Carrier wave

A carrier wave is the original electromagnetic wave (radio wave) that can be transmitted from a radio device that has not yet been modulated.

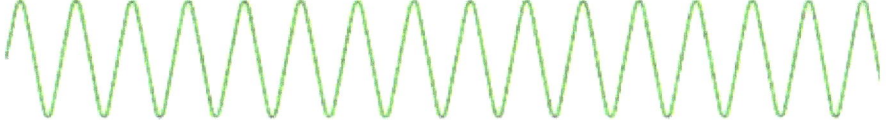

The purpose of the carrier wave is to be modulated (changed) so that it can carry speech, music, images or other signals.

Sometimes when using the radio there may be a problem with the radio unit and when the pilot transmits they transmit the carrier wave only. This means the receiver only hears a constant buzz and no words.

In aviation, the electronic circuitry in the radio unit will change either the Amplitude or the *Frequency* of the carrier wave to carry the embedded signal.

Amplitude Modulation (AM)

If the amplitude is modified to carry a signal it is referred to as Amplitude Modulation or AM radio for short.

The diagram below shows how the amplitude is modified by varying amounts. The radio transmitter and receiver are responsible for coding and decoding this amplitude modulation into understandable words or images.

AM radio is the older technology, where the radio receiver can detect changes in the carrier frequencies amplitude and then amplifies this to drive a speaker. The downside of AM radio is it is influenced by atmospheric conditions and can only carry one embedded signal. The advantage of AM radio over FM radio is that it has a wider frequency band for use and can travel longer distances, especially at night, as the signal will bounce off the ionosphere.

Frequency Modulation (FM)

If the frequency is modified to carry a signal, it is referred to as Frequency Modulation or FM radio for short.

The diagram below shows how the frequency is modified by varying amounts. The radio transmitter and receiver are responsible for coding and decoding this frequency modulation into understandable words or images.

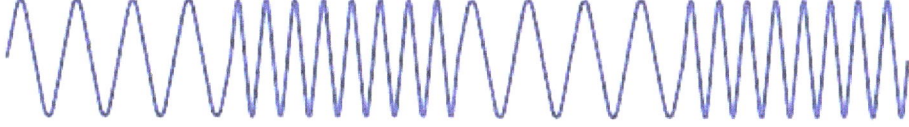

FM radio is the newer technology, where the radio receiver can detect changes in the frequency of a carrier wave with multiple layers of data able to be transmitted giving a stereo or dual-channel signal. Also because most natural electrical interference usually only affects the amplitude of a signal, the FM carrier wave is less likely to be affected by atmospheric disturbances like lightning and water vapour.

The advantage of FM radio over AM radio is it gives a clearer signal and has multiple channels allowing for a stereo sound.

Radio bands

The radio spectrum is divided into various radio bands depending on the frequency. Each particular set of radio frequencies can be used for different applications, as the wavelengths can travel different distances and through different mediums.

The table below describes the radio frequencies able to be transmitted or received in the electromagnetic spectrum.

Band name	Code	Frequency	Wavelength	Examples of uses
Tremendously low frequency	TLF	< 3 Hz	> 100,000 km	Natural and artificial electromagnetic noise such as earthquakes
Extremely low frequency	ELF	3–30 Hz	100,000 km–10,000 km	Communication with submarines
Super low frequency	SLF	30–300 Hz	10,000 km–1000 km	
Ultra-low frequency	ULF	300–3000 Hz	1000 km–100 km	Submarine and underground mine communication
Very low frequency	VLF	3–30k Hz	100 km–10 km	Navigation, time signals, wireless heart rate monitors
Low frequency	LF	30–300 kHz	10km–1km	*NDB navigation aids for aviation*, time signals, AM longwave broadcasting, amateur radio
Medium frequency	MF	300–3000 kHz	1 km–1 metre	*NDB navigation aids for aviation*, AM radio, amateur radio, avalanche beacons
High frequency	HF	3–30 MHz	100 m–10 m	Shortwave broadcasts, citizens band radio, *over the horizon aviation communication*, marine and mobile radiotelephony
Very high frequency	VHF	30–300 MHz	10 m–1 m	FM, television, *line of sight ground to aircraft and aircraft to aircraft communication, aviation navigation aids such as the VOR,*
Ultra-high frequency	UHF	300–3000 MHz	1 m–100 mm	Television, microwave oven, microwave communication, radio astronomy, mobile phones, wireless LAN, Bluetooth, GPS
Super high frequency	SHF	3–30 GHz	100 mm–10 mm	Radio astronomy, microwave communication, wireless LAN, most modern radars, communication satellites, satellite television,
Extremely high frequency	EHF	30–300 GHz	10 mm–1 mm	Radio astronomy, microwave radio relay, microwave remote sensing, directed energy weapon

Aviation Communication and Flight Radio *for Helicopter Pilots*

Band name	Code	Frequency	Wavelength	Examples of uses
Tremendously high frequency	TLF	300–3000 GHz	1 mm–100 um (terahertz)	Medical imaging, computing, sub-mm remote sensing

Aviation bands

In aviation, aircraft typically use the following frequency bands for aviation radios:

- LF and MF
- HF
- VHF, and
- UHF.

Low Frequency (LF) and Medium Frequency (MF)

Low Frequency and Medium Frequency is commonly used by the Non-Directional navigation Beacons (NDB) which can be received by the Automatic Direction Finder (ADF) in the aircraft. This typically operates between 100kHz and 3000kHz.

The ADF will receive not only signals from the NDB but local AM broadcasting stations that transmit in the same bandwidth.

High Frequency (HF)

HF radio is used for long-range communication over the horizon. This is used less and less now as phone and satellite technology is replacing it. The HF radio can transmit and receive signals from other countries around the world. There is a lot of static and it can be difficult to tune and understand.

Very High Frequency (VHF)

VHF radio is used for line of sight ground to aircraft, aircraft-to-ground, and aircraft to aircraft communication.

This is the most commonly used radio band in aviation, with dedicated bandwidth between 118.0 and 135.95MHz where all VHF aircraft transceivers have selector knobs to dial up each frequency which usually comes through very clearly.

VHF radio for the use of the VOR navigation aid with a dedicated frequency band of 108-117.95MHz.

Because VHF radio is line-of-sight, it is affected by altitude. In general, the higher the aircraft flies, the further the transmission can be transmitted and received due to the line of sight becoming better.

Aircraft altitude in feet	VHF coverage in nautical miles
Below 5000 feet AGL	60NM
5000 to 10,000 feet AGL	90NM
Above 10,000 feet AGL	120NM

Ultra High Frequency (UHF)

UHF radio has various applications and uses including:

- GPS, ILS glideslope, International DME, Aircraft transponders, both SSR and ADS-B.
- Line of sight radio communication over short distances.

This is a common frequency used for CB radios, small handhelds or car-based radio systems. It is also used for specialist tasks and by the military on discrete frequencies. It is not a common radio installation in aircraft.

Propagation

Once the radio wave has left the antenna and is transmitted out into the atmosphere, it has the opportunity to be influenced by various obstacles on the way and may travel and take different paths on the way to the receiver. These different paths are referred to as *propagation*.

Radio waves being received by an antenna can be divided into four (4) main categories depending on the path they travelled from the transmitting antenna to the receiving antenna (propagation). They are:

- Direct waves
- Sky waves
- Ground waves; and
- Reflected waves.

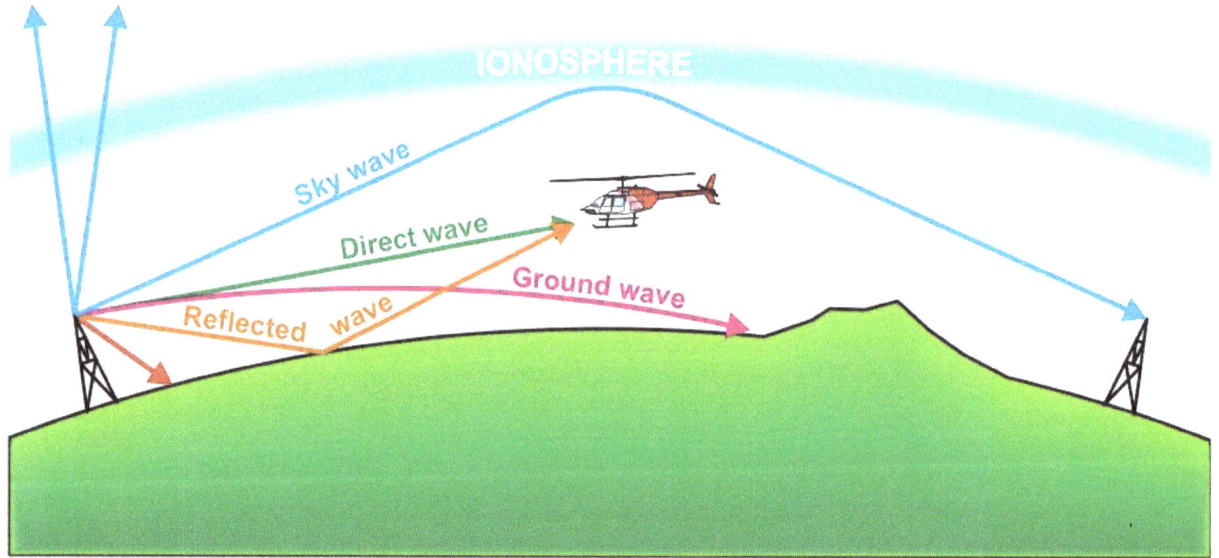

Because radio waves are a form of electromagnetic radiation, they can be influenced by some of the following:

- Variations in water vapour in the troposphere
- Ionisation in the upper atmosphere due to changes in solar activity (solar flares and sunspots)
- Reflection
- Refraction
- Diffraction
- Absorption
- Polarisation
- Scattering, and
- Electromagnetic interference, either from natural sources such as a thunderstorm or other manmade electromagnetic radiation.

Direct waves

Direct waves, also referred to as Space waves, travel directly from the transmitter to the receiver. They will take a direct line of sight are not overly influenced or changed by outside interference.

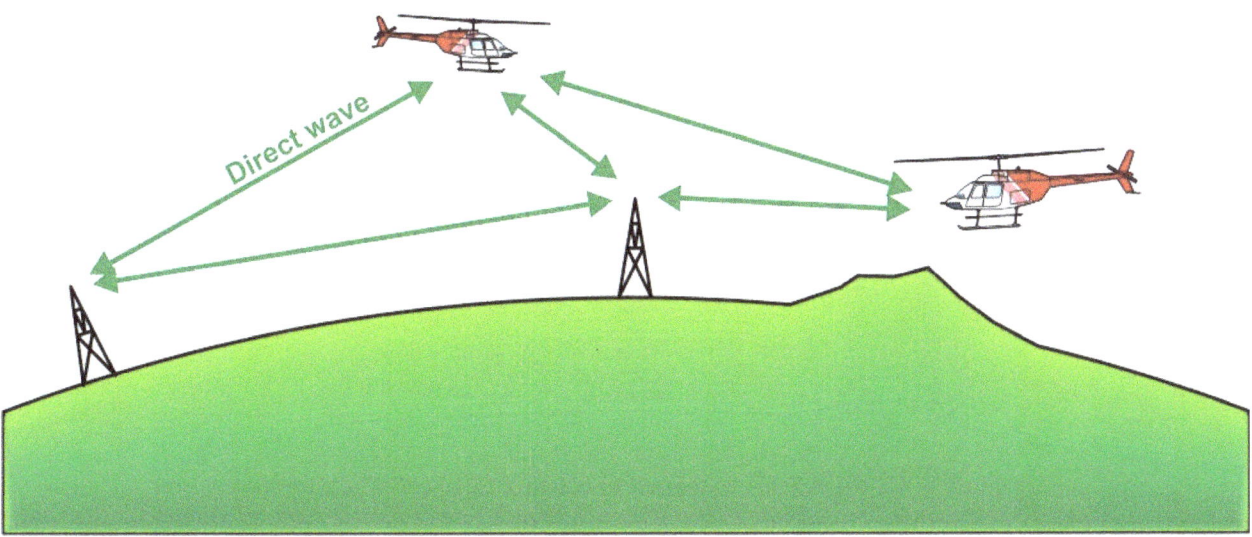

Direct wave is the most common type of radio wave received whilst flying. The VHF (and to some extent UHF) radio is a direct line of sight radio using primarily space or direct waves. This is why, typically, the signal is very clear, because there is less interference.

The disadvantage is the range of the radio is relatively low at lower levels. The higher you are, the longer the range, because the line of sight is greater.

UHF has a short-range, VHF has a longer range.

If you find that you are having difficulty communicating on the radio, it may be because you are too low and the receiver is actually over the horizon. If you climb you may find that the transmission, (both transmitting and receiving) improves.

Line of sight does not mean that you have to be able to see the receiving station; it simply means that there is no solid object between the two stations. VHF radio will go through cloud as if it was not there; it will not go through a mountain.

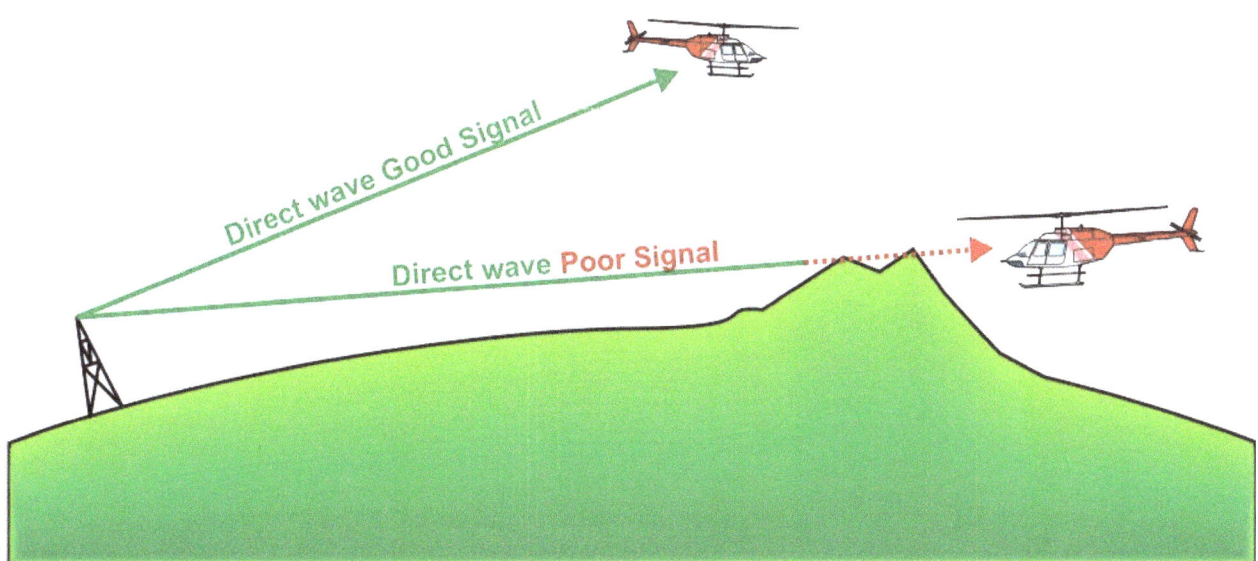

Sky waves

Once the radio wave is transmitted, it will radiate outwards in all directions equally. Its path (propagation) will change depending on what object, surface or medium it then encounters.

Once the signal reaches the ionosphere, it will be affected depending on its frequency.

The VHF radio wave will go right through the ionosphere and continue into space.

The HF radio and any frequency bands below the HF range will be subjected to varying amounts of absorption and reflection by the ionosphere, depending on the ionospheres state at the time. These radio waves can then be reflected or modified in some way and will then come back down into the atmosphere where they will be received in their modified state.

It is important to note that not all sky waves return to the earth, some are completely absorbed by the ionosphere and some will continue out into space.

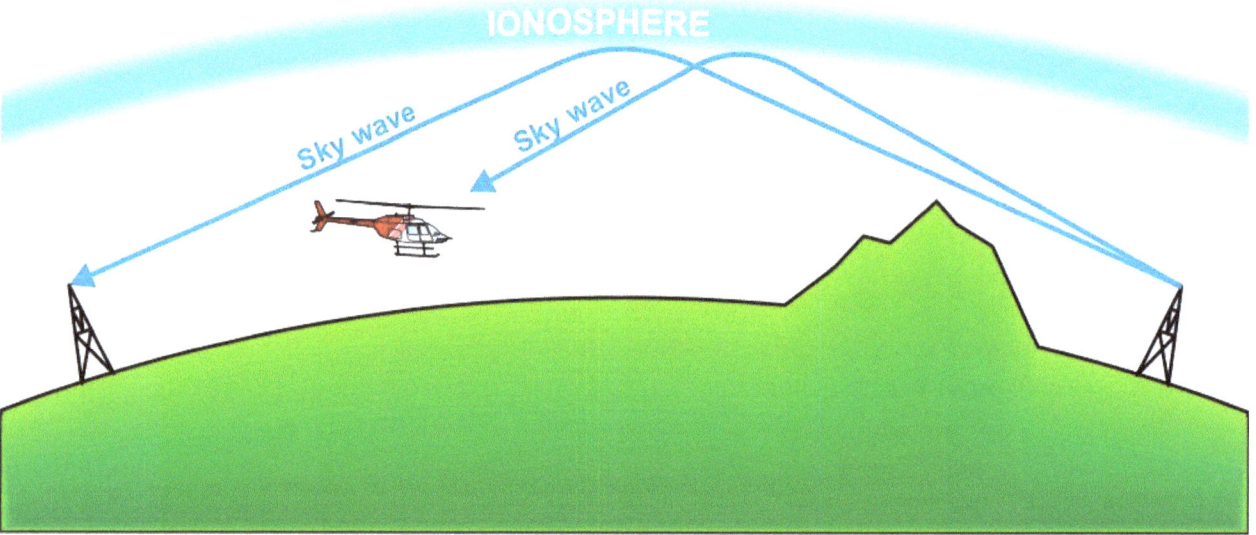

The big advantage of HF radio is that the Skywave can be used to transmit signals a very long distance over the horizon. The disadvantage is there is a lot of interference and the frequency can change as the ionosphere changes so the antenna will have to be constantly "tuned" to accept the incoming signal.

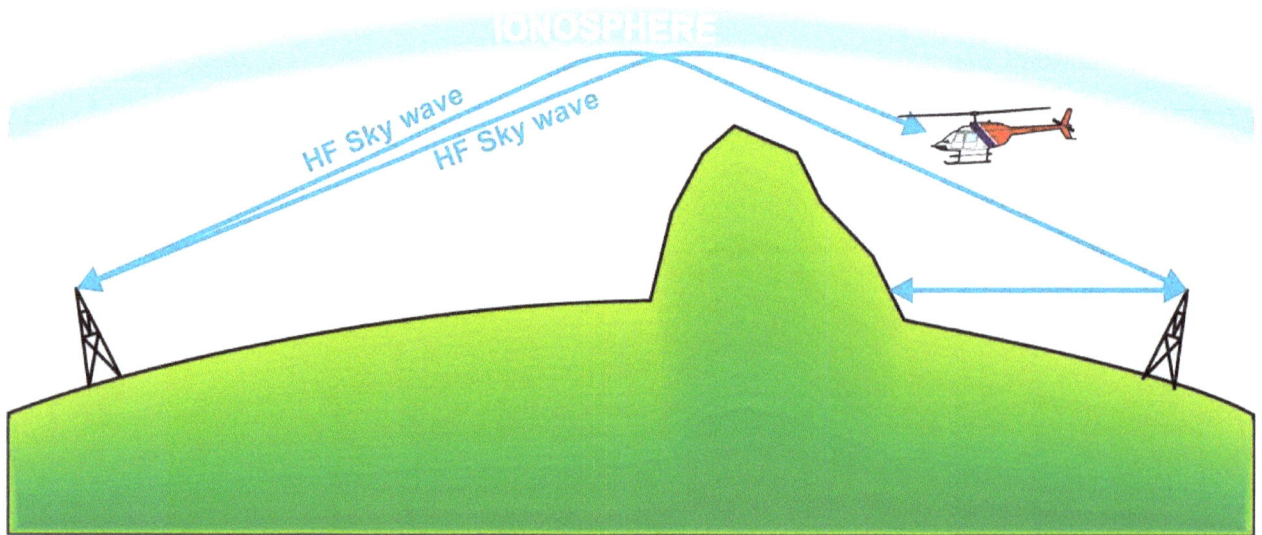

Ground waves

A ground or surface wave follows a path very close to the surface of the earth and approximately parallel to it. It does not leave the earth's lower atmosphere and it is this difference that separates it from a sky wave.

Ground waves enable communication in the MF band out to approximately 160KMs.

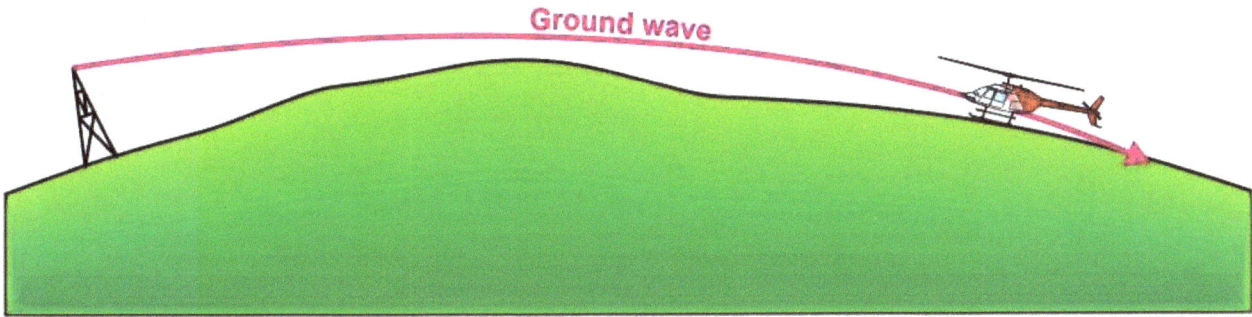

Because the ground wave is travelling very close to the surface, it can be influenced by the varying densities in the atmosphere, obstacles such as mountains and buildings as well as atmospheric disturbances, particularly lightning in thunderstorms.

A good example of a ground wave is the NDB. When on the ground, tune in an NDB that is out over the horizon, but within say 100kms. You should receive the signal and also have the ADF indicator point to the station. Once the helicopter lifts off the ground, the ground wave can no longer be received by the radio and you will lose the signal. Since thunderstorms affect ground waves, ADFs will also be affected by thunderstorms.

Reflected waves

Reflected radio waves are normal direct waves that have come into contact with a surface that reflects them back into the atmosphere or reflects them to an antenna. There may also be a time delay in the signal as it has taken a longer path to get to the receiver, while the direct wave has gone directly from transmitter to receiver.

If the waves have been reflected from a surface, such as water, or snow, a mountain or a man-made object etc., then some of the signal may be slightly changed which we would hear as interference.

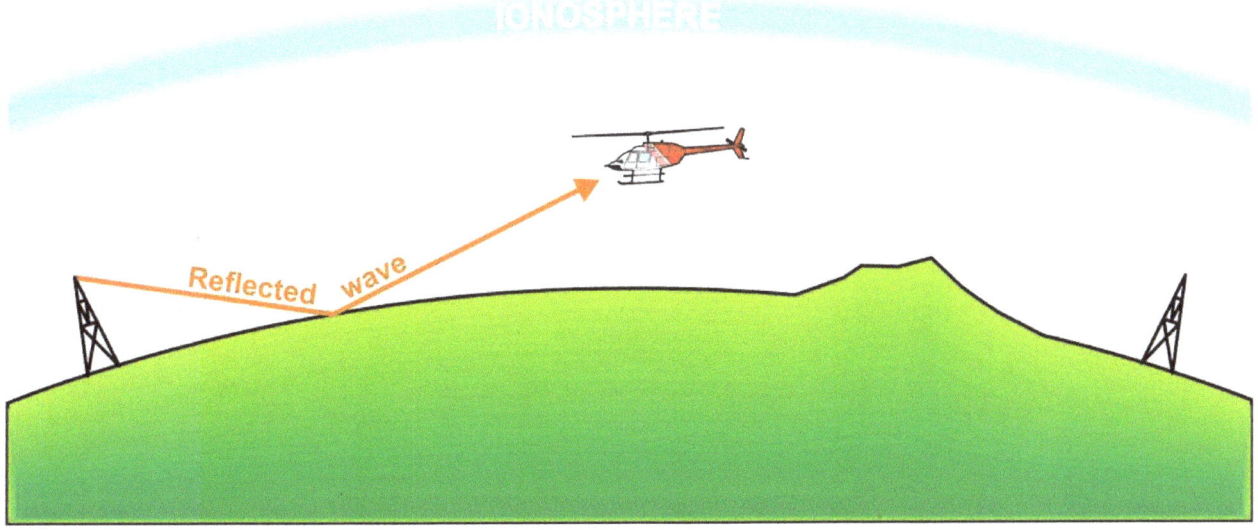

If the radio wave is collected in something like a satellite dish, then the signal may be amplified and through processors cleaned up to eventually give a clearer signal as more of the radio signal is received.

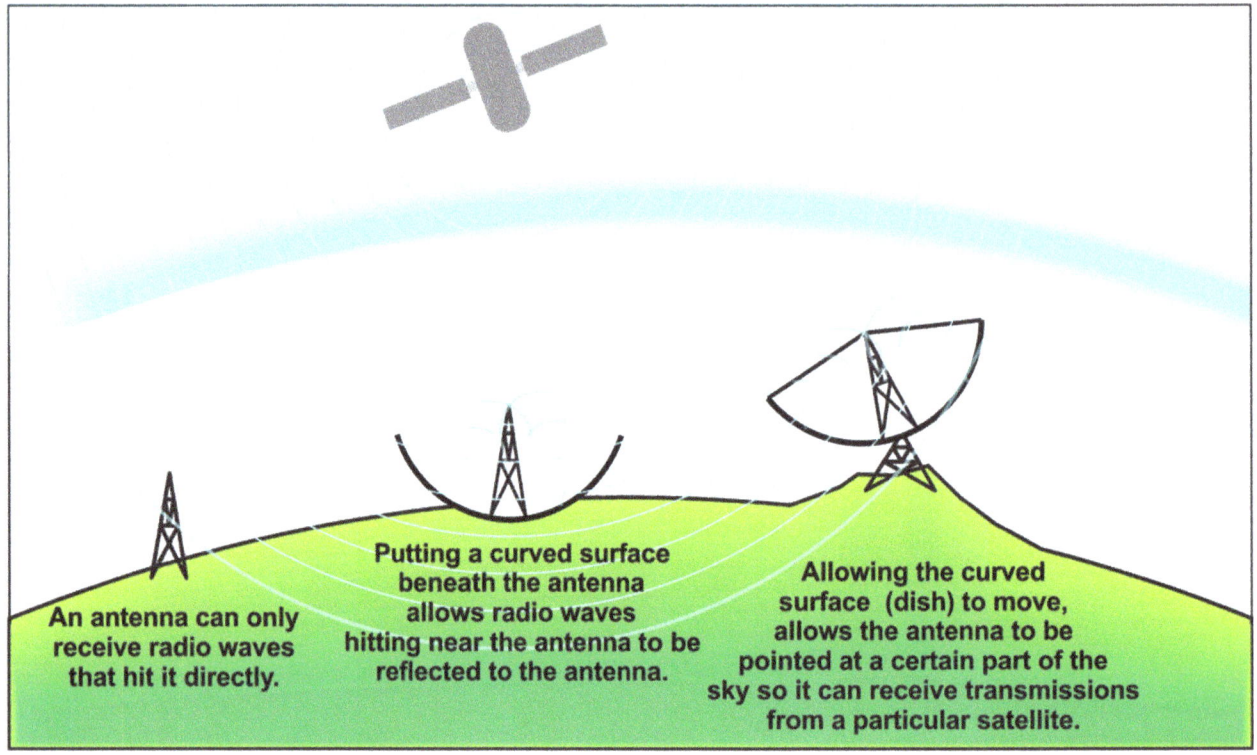

Explaining wave interference

To better understand what happens to a radio wave when it is disturbed, we need to go back to the rock in the water example.

Consider the rock being thrown in the water and waves spreading out from the centre. Now imagine another set of waves from another source interfering with the original waves. They will now be cancelled out, bent, reflected or in some other way affected.

The same goes for radio waves if they hit something as they travel, they will be absorbed, reflected, bent or split up. This will cause interference with the signal and make it harder to hear or understand.

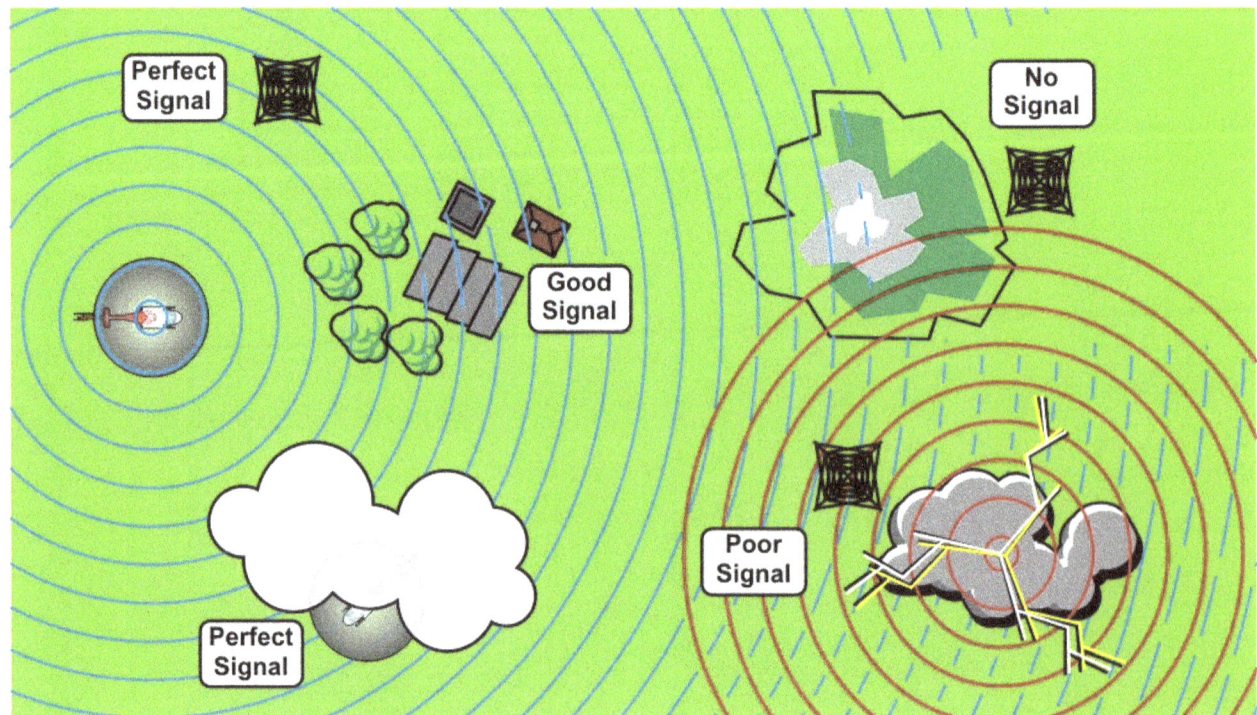

Aviation Communication and Flight Radio *for Helicopter Pilots*

Know Your Equipment

Aim

This chapter aims to introduce the trainee to the aircraft's radios and how to:

- identify each one
- operate, tune, identify and test each radio, and then
- make and receive transmissions.

Introduction

There are a large number of different radio types and designs that may be installed in aircraft. It is up to the pilot to fully understand how the particular model/s in your aircraft will work and how to operate them. There is nothing better than actually sitting in the aircraft and playing with all the radios and the various functions. Reading about them will only give you so much knowledge. Using them is the key to becoming proficient.

In general, all radio equipment has many of the same features and operating knobs, but they may be in different locations and operated slightly differently. Each piece of equipment has a particular function and a good understanding by the pilot by *memory* is essential. There is no time to read a manual on how to use radios when flying. Using the radios has to be automatic and instinctive.

It is also important to realize that the helmet or headset plays a vital role in operating the radio, so it will be included in this chapter as part of the radio system.

In general, all radio systems require the following to operate:

- Microphone and speakers to turn sound into electrical signals and electrical signals back into sound
- ON/OFF switch which controls power to the system
- Volume control can be adjusted depending on the crews' requirements
- Squelch control which allows the background interference noise to be filtered out
- Channel selector knobs to change frequency; and
- Display screen that shows what frequency is currently in use or about to be used.

Bell206BIII Radio Stack

The radio stack in a Becker Helicopters Bell 206BIII is made up of the audio panel, the Garmin 430, a Bendix/King KY196A VHF transceiver, a Bendix/King KR87 ADF navigation aid and a Transponder.

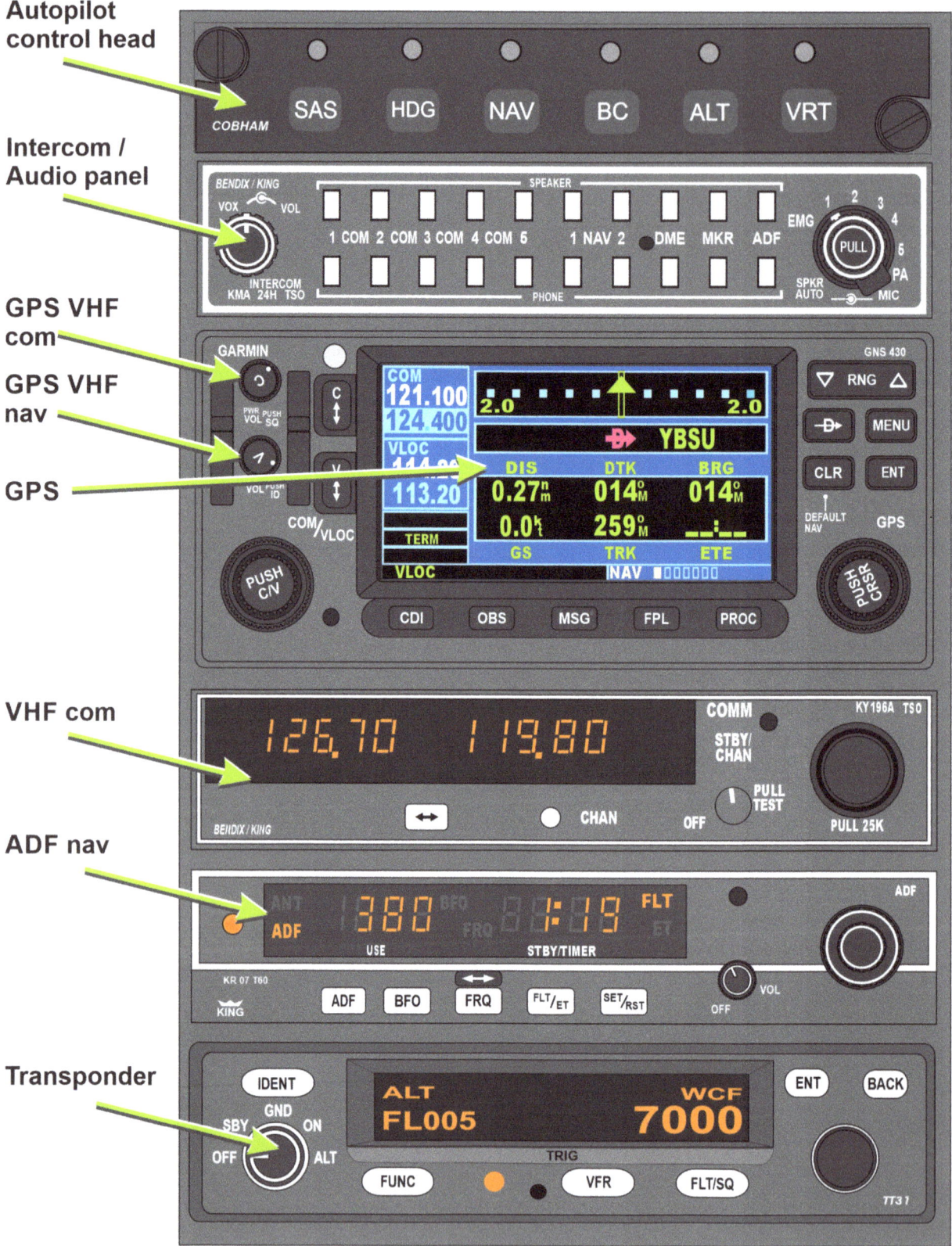

Aviation Communication and Flight Radio *for Helicopter Pilots*

HeliSAS Autopilot Control Head

Although HeliSAS Autopilot Control Head is not a radio, it is installed on the top of the radio stack and is worth mentioning here.

This is the control head that allows the pilot to select:

1. **SAS**: Stability Augmentation System ON / OFF. Pressing this button activates the force trim and readies the autopilot to accept the other functions.
2. **HDG**: Heading guidance ON / OFF. Pressing this button allows the heading bug to control the autopilot.
3. **NAV**: Navigation guidance ON / OFF. Pressing this button allows the selected navigation feature (GPS or VOR) to control the autopilot.
4. **BC**: Back course function is not connected.
5. **ALT**: Altitude hold ON / OFF: Pressing this button allows the autopilot to maintain the current altitude.
6. **VRT**: Vertical guidance ON / OFF: Pressing this button when the NAV button is also pressed allows the ILS to give vertical guidance to the autopilot when on an approach.
7. Above each button is a LED light. If the LED light is white, then the unit is on standby.

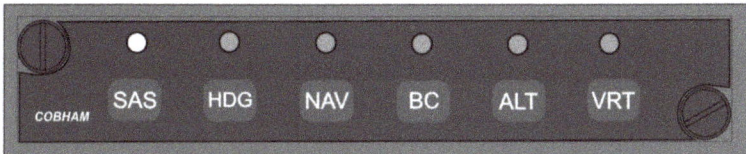

8. If the LED light is green, then the unit is active.

Mike Becker, Becker Helicopters

Audio Panel

The audio panel is the central unit that all other radios are connected to.

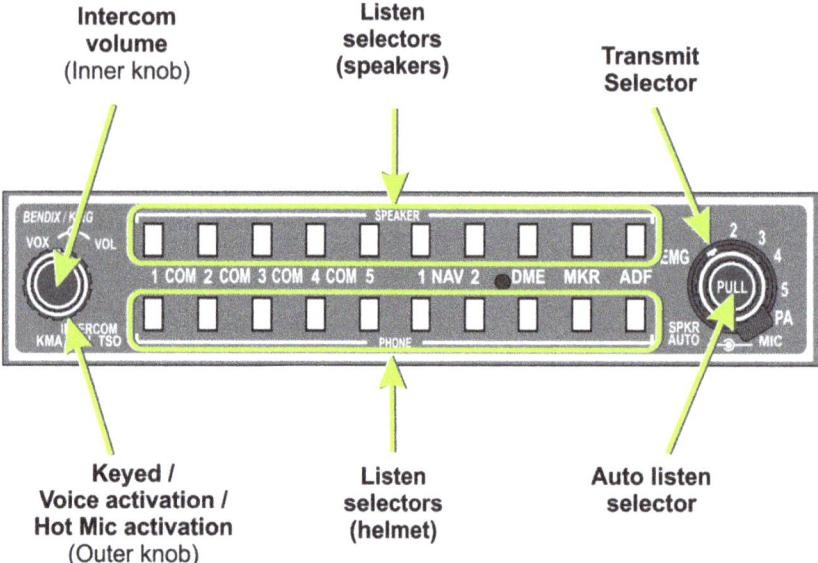

It allows the crew to do the following:

1. Talk to each other via the intercom system and adjust the VOX (voice-activated transmission) sensitivity and volume of the intercom system.
2. Select individual or multiple radios to listen to, and then transmit either through an external speaker or through a headset or helmet.
3. Select the different navigation aids audio functions so that they can be identified.
4. Select EMG so that the audio panel circuitry can be bypassed in the event the audio unit fails. This allows the crew to transmit directly through COMM 1 on the selected frequency.
5. Adjust the microphone sensitivity with the VOX knob, allowing the crew to set either a "Hot Mic," a "VOX" position or a "Keyed Mic" position.

    (a) **Hot Mic**

    When the VOX selector knob is rotated all the way to the right the intercom microphone will always be activated. The advantage is all crew members can talk at the same time to each other like a normal conversation. The disadvantage is it is often distractingly loud and can be confusing with everyone talking at the same time. It also means there is a lot of background noise that is constantly being delivered to the speakers in the helmet.

    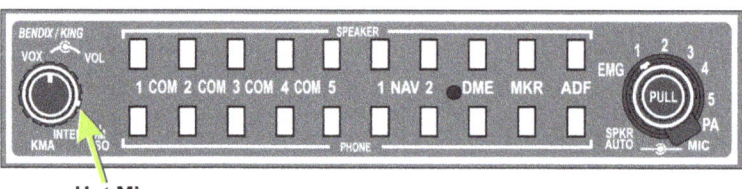
    Hot Mic Position

    (b) **VOX position**

    The crew can adjust the VOX sensitivity so that the intercom is not activated when no one is talking, but when someone does talk then the microphone automatically turns itself on as it is voice-activated. This is the best position for the VOX to be in, as the crew does not have to constantly pull the Intercom To Talk (ITT) trigger to talk, but when no one is talking the system is quiet and all the background noise is filtered out.

VOX Range

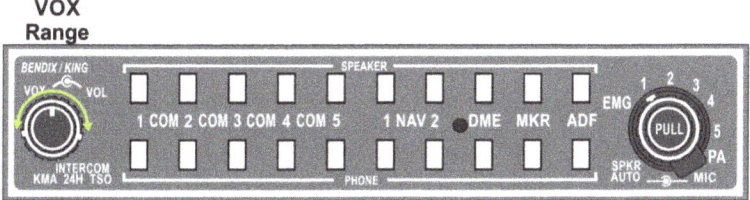

(c) **Keyed Mic**

In some situations the VOX cannot work, this is particularly relevant when flying with the doors off or when there is excessive external noise to the point that the VOX cannot cope. In this instance, the crew can turn the VOX knob all the way to the left until it clicks OFF. At that point, the VOX is deactivated and the crew now must key the ITT whenever they want to talk on the intercom

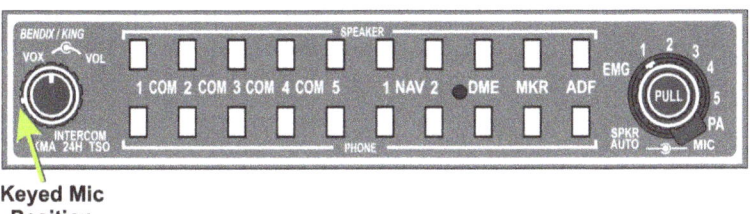

Keyed Mic Position

Garmin GPS/NAV/COMM

The Garmin 430 GPS Navigation Transceiver is a multi-faceted device. It has three separate systems that all interface and are operated by one unit.

- First, it is a GPS that is used for navigation and instrument approaches with an updated database of information.
- Second, it is a VHF transceiver that is designated as the COMM 1; and
- Thirdly, it is a VOR radio navigation aid.

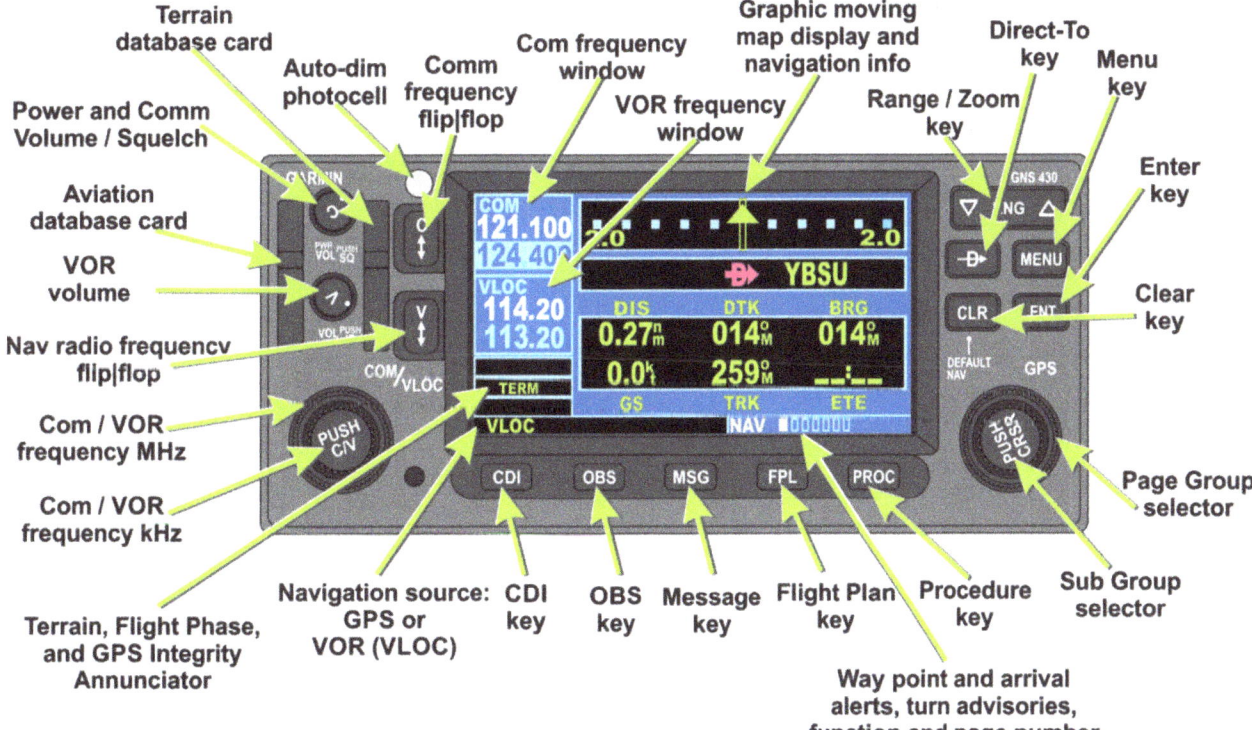

COMM 2

The Bendix/King KY196A is a dedicated VHF transceiver that is designated as the COMM 2. Its sole purpose is as a second VHF radio.

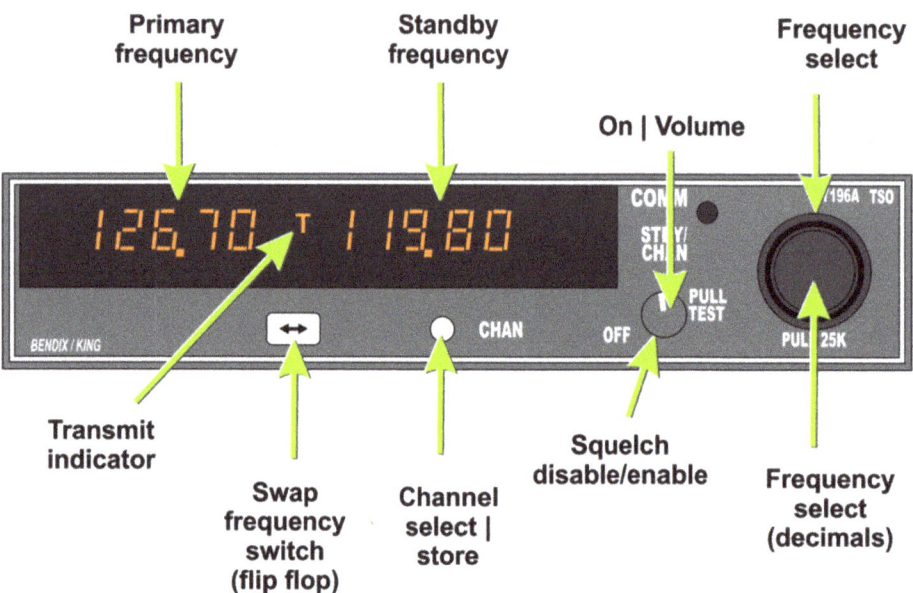

Automatic Direction Finding (ADF)

The Bendix/King KR87 ADF navigation aid is used as a radio navigation aid, it also has a stopwatch and timer function.

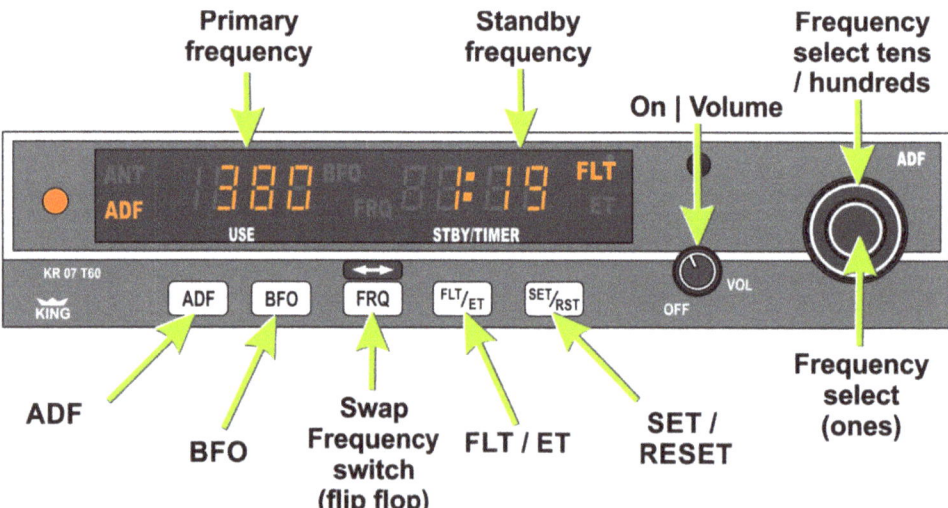

Transponder

The transponder is a secondary surveillance radar (SSR) device that allows ATC to see the aircraft on their radar screens. The same signals sent out for the ATC radar are also used by TCAS (Traffic Collision Avoidance Systems) in other aircraft.

The IDENT button is used by the pilot when ATC request that it be pressed. When pressing the IDENT button, the transponder will send out a short burst of radar pulses that allows ATC to positively identify the helicopter.

The words used by ATC when requesting the IDENT button to be pressed are as follows:

"WCF, Brisbane Centre Squawk IDENT"
    "Squawk IDENT WCF"
"WCF, identified confirm altitude"
    "Maintaining 6500 WCF"

Each aircraft will be given a discrete code that may change on every flight based on the category of operation and which airspace the aircraft will be operating in. If aircraft are not given a discrete code by ATC, then one of the following standard codes shall be used until otherwise advised.

Code	Description	
1200	VFR in G and E Airspace	
2000	IFR in G airspace	
3000	VFR in A, C and D airspace IFR in E airspace	
4000	SAR greater than 15NM offshore in G airspace	
7500	Hijack *(75 taken alive)*	*Hi Jack...*
7600	Radio failure *(76 need a fix)*	*I can't talk right now...*
7700	General emergency *(77 going to heaven)*	*I have an emergency...*

Mike Becker, Becker Helicopters

There are two common types of transponder currently in use; they are the old-style Mode C transponder and the newer Mode S Transponder.

1. The Mode C transponder will give ATC the ability to estimate the helicopters position and pressure altitude, but it has no other features.

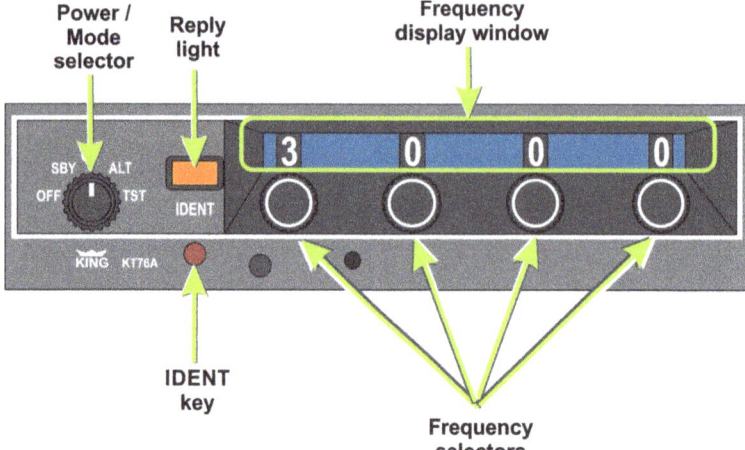

2. The GTRIG Mode S transponder will give position and Pressure Altitude and give the identity of the helicopter. ATC will see the registration and be able to identify you directly. Mode S transponders also have a digital screen that will give the pilot information such as pressure altitude and current altitude, as well as access to additional functions and features including a stopwatch and timer.

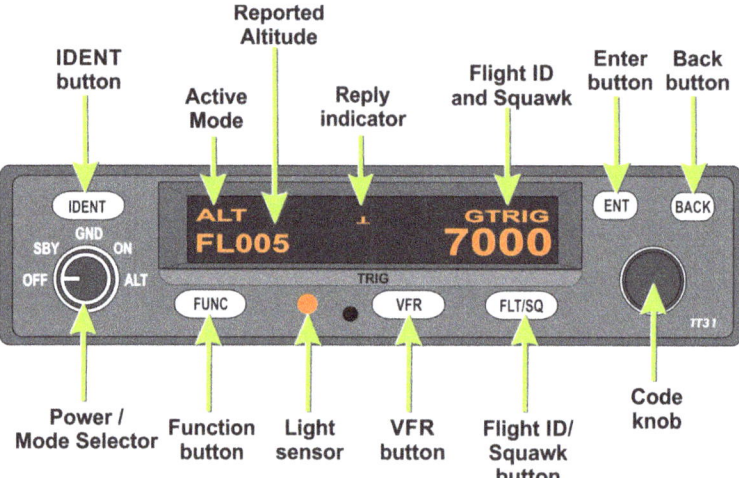

Traffic Collision Avoidance System (TCAS)

The Traffic Collision Avoidance System or TCAS is an electronic device installed in the helicopter that will receive signals from a transponder unit from another aircraft. It will then display this information onto a screen in the cockpit so that the crew can see where any conflicting traffic may be. It is not usually installed in smaller aircraft due to the expense, but it is installed on all airliners and more sophisticated modern aircraft. It is becoming more common, as Electronic Flight Information Systems (EFIS) becomes more common.

Often the TCAS is also connected to a voice generator that will give an aural alert, as well as display on the screen when traffic is close.

If the unit detects another aircraft on a collision course or within a pre-set distance from your aircraft, it will activate the aural generator and you will hear the warning message:

"TRAFFIC TRAFFIC"

The conflicting traffic will then show up as a small triangle or circle of various colours depending on:

- the other aircraft's proximity, and
- whether it is coming towards you or going away.

Each circle or triangle will also have a + or – with a number indicating how many feet above or below the other aircraft is in relation to your aircraft in hundreds (x 100) of feet.

> **Example**
>
> For example, +2 means the other aircraft is 200 feet above you. -20 means the other aircraft is 2000 feet below you. +05 means the other aircraft is 500 feet above you.

Many helicopters are not fitted with any TCAS system, **BUT** it is very important that the helicopters transponder is always ON in-flight so that other aircraft that do have TCAS can detect you.

Interfacing with the radios

Headset and helmet

The headset or helmet plugs directly into the aircraft's radio system and allows the pilot to pull a "trigger" or "key" on the cyclic to activate the transmit button on the radio.

The pilot will speak into a microphone so that the voice can be converted into an electrical current that is then transmitted by the radio.

The microphone is unidirectional (one direction). That means it only receives signals from one direction. For this reason, it must be positioned very close to the mouth as it is designed not to pick up all the extra external noise in the cockpit. If it is positioned too far away from the mouth, or not directly in front of the mouth, the pilot's words cannot be received by the microphone. As a guide, the microphone should be approximately 0.5cm to 1cm away from your mouth.

Good microphone position

Bad microphone position

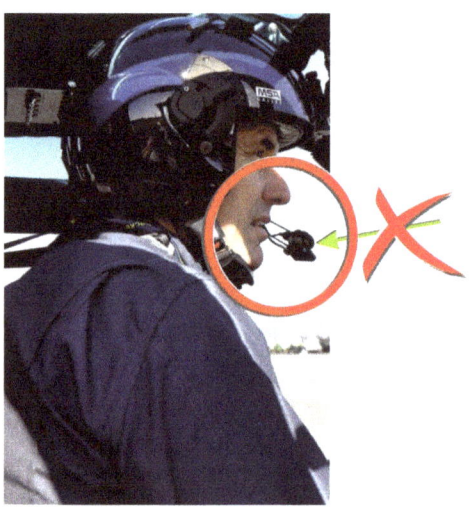

Most headsets or helmets also have a volume control that the wearer can use to turn their volume up or down. In a multi-crew environment, this is very important, as each crew member may be receiving the volume of the intercom and radios at different levels due to differences in the aircraft wiring and headset or helmet configurations, as well as their personal hearing tolerances and choice of earplug.

The volume control may be installed directly on the helmet as a small knob or may be attached to the cable. Both can be adjusted by the wearer to fine-tune the volume.

Helmet volume

Helmet cable volume

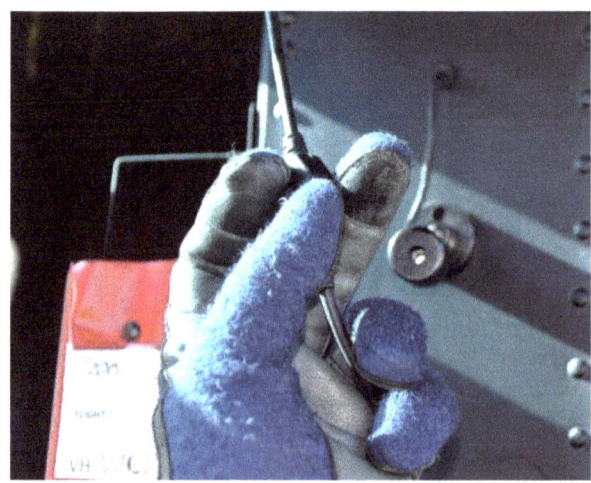

Switches

Additional to the actual radios, there may be other switches and circuit breakers that are designed to protect the avionics equipment, this includes:

1. **Master Battery switch.**

   Often referred to as simply the Battery Switch turns on the electrical supply from the batteries to the aircraft. The only exception to this is if the aircraft is on the ground and it has an external power supply. No radios will operate unless it has an electrical supply, which usually means the Master Battery Switch needs to be set to BAT which indicates that it is ON.

2. **Radio Master or Avionics Master switch**

   Most modern helicopters have an Avionics Master switch. This allows the radios to always remain in the ON position within the radio stack. The Radio Master switch will be turned ON after start or OFF before shutdown and will thus turn all the radios ON or OFF at the same time.

   The Radio Master switch is there to protect the avionics system from electrical spikes that may happen when turning the master battery switch ON or OFF and when starting, it is also there as a convenience so that the crew only have one switch to turn ON or OFF instead of each individual radio.

   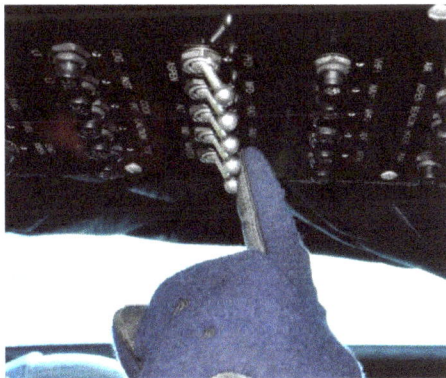

3. **Circuit breakers.**

   Circuit breakers are designed to protect electrical circuits in the event something goes wrong electrically. If a radio has an electrical short, instead of that short causing a fire or further damaging the radio equipment, the circuit breaker will reach a load limit and then POP out. Additionally, if a radio has a problem and starts smoking or heating up while in flight, the pilot can pull out the circuit breaker to take away all electrical current to that particular radio. If a circuit breaker has popped OUT, then it is protecting the radio and is doing its job. When it is popped OUT, there is no electrical current flowing to the radio.

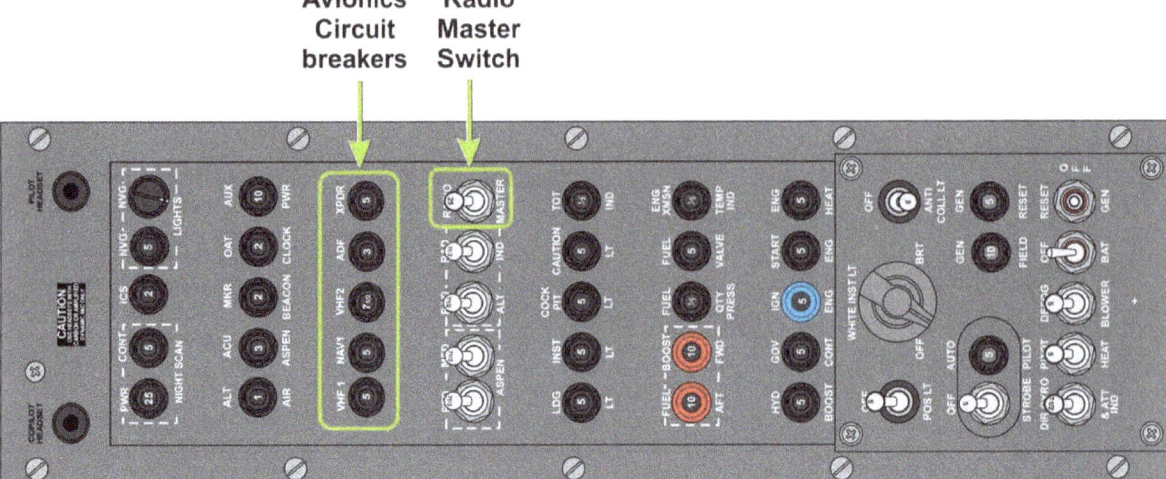

4. **PTT and ITT**

   On the cyclic, there is a trigger mechanism that the pilot must press to activate the microphone when transmitting on the radio. This is called the **P**ress **T**o **T**alk (PTT) button.

   It has two (2) positions. One-click at halfway will activate the intercom and two clicks when pulled all the way will activate the radio.

   When only pulling it one click to activate the intercom, this is referred to as the **I**ntercom **T**o **T**alk (ITT) position.

Trigger released	ITT trigger position	PTT trigger position
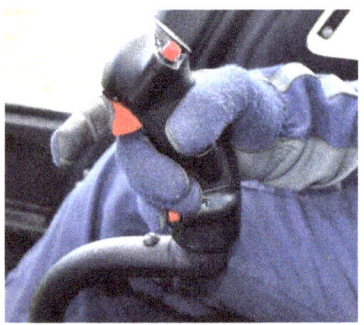	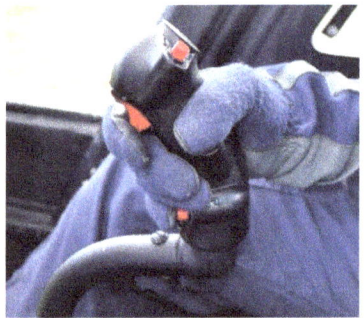	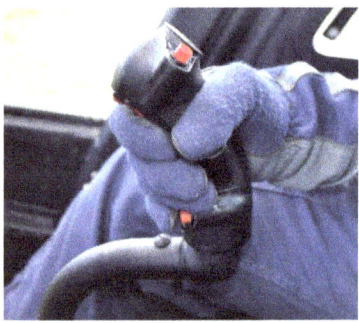

There is a second PTT/ITT on the second cyclic and a third PTT on the floor that the instructor can press with his foot so that he does not have to hold the cyclic while the trainee is flying.

PTT Co-pilot Cyclic

PTT Co-pilot foot switch

Summary

It is important, as a pilot that you get to know your equipment.

One way to do this is to, before flying, sit in the helicopter and turn on the radios. Experiment with all the knobs, buttons and switches; adjust the various volumes and squelches.

Take out some of your training notes and go through each setting on the radios.

A word of caution

When turning on the battery to activate the radios without the engine going, the battery will go flat within 30-45 minutes and the helicopter will, therefore, not be able to be started.

If you want to practice with the radios, then consult with your instructor.

References

FAA.gov. (2017). *Air traffic controllers at the Washington ARTCC*. Wikimedia Commons (Public Domain). https://commons.wikimedia.org/wiki/File:Air_traffic_controllers_at_the_Washington_ARTCC.jpg

Jpatokal. (2009). *Route map of the world's scheduled commercial airline traffic, 2009*. Wikimedia Commons (CC 3.0). https://en.wikipedia.org/wiki/Commercial_aviation#/media/File:World-airline-routemap-2009.png

Landesman, E. (2010). *LAX-elal-takeoff*. Wikimedia Commons (CC 3.0). https://commons.wikimedia.org/wiki/File:LAX-elal-takeoff.jpg

redlegsfan21. (2013). *Hartsfield-Jackson Atlanta International Airport*. Wikimedia Commons (CC 2.0). https://commons.wikimedia.org/wiki/File:Hartsfield-Jackson_Atlanta_International_Airport_(7039222923).jpg

Abbreviations

The following abbreviations are used in this book.

Abbreviation	Title
ACD	Airways Clearance Delivery
ADF	Automatic direction finding equipment
AIP	Aeronautical Information Package from Airservices Australia
ATIS	Automatic Terminal Information Service
B206BIII	Bell 206 BIII Jet Ranger
CASA	Civil Aviation Safety Authority of Australia
CASR	Civil Aviation Safety Regulations
COMM	Communications
CTA	Control Area
CTAF	Common Traffic Advisory Frequency
CTR	Control Zone
ERSA	En Route Supplement Australia from Airservices Australia
FAA	Federal Aviation Administration, the US aviation regulator.
FIR	Flight Instructor Rating
FROL	Flight Radio Operators Licence
GPS	Global Positioning System
Hz	Hertz
ICAO	International Civil Aviation Organisation
IFR	Instrument Flight Rules
ITT	Intercom To Talk
km	Kilometres
kt	Knots
NAV	Navigation
nm	Nautical miles
NOTAM	Notice to Airmen
OCTA	Outside Controlled Airspace

Abbreviation	Title
PTT	Press To Talk
RCC	Rescue Co-ordination Centre
TCAS	Traffic Alert and Collision Avoidance System
UHF	Ultra High Frequency
VFG	Visual Flight Guide from CASA
VFR	Visual Flight Rules
VHF	Very High Frequency
VNC	Visual Navigation Chart
VOX	Voice activated transmission
VTC	Visual Terminal Chart